First published in 2017 by RSC Enterprise Ltd, 3 Chapel Lane, Stratford-upon-Avon, Warwickshire CV37 6BE.

www.rsc.org.uk

ISBN: 978-0-9568012-1-0

A catalogue record for this book is available from the British Library.

IMAGE CREDITS
Cover image by Andy Williams. Sam Allard p79 (clr), 83, 96-97; Lucy Barriball 32, 34 (guitar), 91; Donald Cooper 98-103; Andrew Fox 116, 120-21; Rob Freeman 88; Manuel Harlan 40-45, 132-135, 139 (exc. Shubert); Stewart Hemley 80-82, 84, 90, 119; Ellie Kurttz 46-57, 104-115; Richard Lakos 85-87 (exc. Joanne); Katherine Leedale 87 (Joanne); Topher McGrillis 20-30, 122-130; Jill Marcus 139 (Shubert); Helen Maybanks 4, 36-39, 58-75; Keith Pattison 10-13, 16; James Phillips 76-79 (b/w); Liu Qi 15 (Peking Opera); David Tett 33-35 (exc. guitar & Mimbre), 92 (bottom), 142-3; Yin Xuefeng 18.

All images © RSC except: p15 NCPA © Sihasakprachum courtesy Sihasakprachum/Shutterstock.com, Peking Opera © SDAC, Tiananmen gate © Taras Vyshnya/Shutterstock.com, Brooklyn Bridge © Sergio TB courtesy Sergio TB/Shutterstock.com, Great Wall © aphotostory/Shutterstock.com; 18 © SDAC; 34 Mimbre photo © Mimbre; 76-79 (b/w) © Slung Low; 87 Joanne © Katherine Leedale; 92 (top) © Number 10 Downing Street; 92 (WSC) © David Tett; 132-135 © RSC/CFT.

THE BIG YEAR

2016 – A VERY SPECIAL YEAR IN THE LIFE OF THE ROYAL SHAKESPEARE COMPANY

I've often said that Shakespeare has been a passport through my life. My actual passport came up for renewal in 2016, so imagine my delight when a parcel arrived from HM Passport Office containing the newly designed British passport with a 3D watermark of Shakespeare's face embedded on every visa page! The new passport celebrates the 'Creative United Kingdom', so among portraits of John Constable, John Harrison, and the work of contemporary artists Anish Kapoor and Antony Gormley, are iconic images of Stephenson's Rocket and the Penny Black. But another surprise awaits. For here, celebrating Great British architecture, is our own Elisabeth Scott, the architect of the 1932 Shakespeare Memorial Theatre in Stratford-upon-Avon. Her face is unfamiliar to many, but here she is in a natty cloche hat, and behind her is an image of the Royal Shakespeare Theatre in its 2010 iteration.

Yes, as expected, Shakespeare was everywhere in 2016. The Post Office brought out a special set of stamps with quotations from the plays, and The Royal Mint produced a set of three brilliant uncirculated Shakespeare £2 coins, with images of Yorick's skull, a dagger and crown, and a jester's hat and marotte. There was even a Shakespeare-themed *Countryfile* on the BBC.

Here in Stratford the whole town rose to the occasion of its most famous son's jubilee. The Shakespeare Birthplace Trust opened its splendid new redevelopment of New Place, the site of the home Shakespeare bought in 1597; and King Edward VI School, Shakespeare's alma mater, opened its schoolroom to the public, reminding me of the story of the pupil who, when told that Shakespeare was born and died on the same day, asked 'How did he manage to write so many plays then?'

At the RSC, our goal for 2016 was to introduce as many new faces as we could to Shakespeare, and to our work. To this end, we mounted our first international tour to the People's Republic of China with productions from our main repertoire, and undertook a residency in New York at the Brooklyn Academy of Music. We created a very special production of *A Midsummer Night's Dream* to tour the nine regions and four nations of the UK, with amateur actors playing Bottom and the Rude Mechanicals, and local schoolchildren playing Titania's fairies. We joined forces with the BBC to present *Shakespeare Live! From the RSC* on Shakespeare's birthday, which celebrated his legacy in opera, jazz, ballet, rap and musical theatre, with contributions from a host of stars, and our President Prince Charles in the audience.

In the Royal Shakespeare Theatre, we continued our journey through the folio of Shakespeare's plays (we are already just over a third of our way through the canon since we launched the series with *Richard II* in 2013), creating new productions of *Hamlet*, *Cymbeline* and *King Lear*, and a special innovative production of *The Tempest* with Intel and The Imaginarium Studios. All these productions were broadcast live across the world and streamed for free into schools across the country through our Live From Stratford-upon-Avon initiative.

Meanwhile, in the Swan this summer, we marked the 400th anniversary of Cervantes' death (he died on the same date as Shakespeare) with a new production of *Don Quixote*, and the 400th anniversary of the publication of Ben Jonson's First Folio with a production of

Left:
Judi Dench,
Al Murray

5

The Alchemist, adding a production of *Doctor Faustus* by Christopher Marlowe, another of Shakespeare's great contemporaries and possibly also one of his collaborators, as we learned this year.

In the autumn we celebrated the Swan Theatre's 30th birthday with the two plays that opened the theatre in 1986: Shakespeare and John Fletcher's *The Two Noble Kinsmen* and Aphra Behn's *The Rover*, and played them in repertoire with a new play by Anders Lustgarten, *The Seven Acts of Mercy.*

For good measure, we also reopened The Other Place (TOP) and held a summer festival of new work, *Making Mischief,* that consisted of four exciting radical plays: *Fall of the Kingdom, Rise of the Foot Soldier* by Somalia Seaton, *Always Orange* by Fraser Grace, a revival of Alice Birch's *Revolt. She Said. Revolt Again.* and finally *Joanne,* in conjunction with Clean Break Theatre Company. The creative hub that is The Other Place now proudly houses three marvellous new rehearsal rooms, a studio theatre, and a great cafe, as well as our fabulous costume-hire wardrobe.

Our Education department went from strength to strength, mounting a schools' Playmaking Festival at TOP; a special schools' event at 10 Downing Street in the presence of the then Prime Minister David Cameron; and celebrated a decade of the Learning and Performance Network in the Swan.

We collaborated with three innovative companies: Mimbre delighted audiences around Shakespeare's birthday with an open-air Shakespeare show; Slung Low created a magical midsummer event in the Avonbank gardens; and Stan's Cafe invented a Shakespeare journey around town.

The image used in the watermarks of the new 2016 version of the UK Passport is taken from the Chandos portrait of Shakespeare. And it was a great honour for us to welcome this famous painting to Stratford-upon-Avon for the opening of our new exhibition *The Play's The Thing,* in the splendidly refurbished Swan Wing in October. The painting came on loan from the National Portrait Gallery, where it is catalogued as NPG1, being the first acquisition the gallery ever made when it opened in 1856.

So, it really has been a *big year.* This book marks what's been a very special series of events in the Company's history, and celebrates the extraordinary team of people who made them happen.

I hope we have gone some way to achieving our goal, and inspired more and more people, proving that engaging with Shakespeare can provide a passport through their lives. He runs like a watermark through all our work, constantly present, identifying a standard of excellence and inspiring us to achieve it.

Gregory Doran

Gregory Doran, Artistic Director

The RSC Acting Companies are generously supported by THE GATSBY CHARITABLE FOUNDATION and THE KOVNER FOUNDATION.

The work of the RSC Literary Department is generously supported by THE DRUE HEINZ TRUST.

So much had to happen behind the scenes to make the productions and events described in this book possible. It all required many and varied skills, talent, thought, detailed planning, problem solving, heavy lifting, and continual hard work, each in abundance. We always remember that the RSC is a charity, producing theatre at its best, sharing that as widely as possible and, in doing so, transforming lives and communities.

In order to realise productions from the imaginations of our creative teams to the stage, our workshops in Stratford-upon-Avon have designed, created and painted sets ranging from the heaviest metal to the lightest mosquito netting – and almost everything in between. Costumes (from full evening dress to fantastical creatures), hats, gloves, shoes and armour have been individually made and fitted; wigs made and dressed; make-up applied; props selected; special effects imagined and implemented; band rooms created; musical scores written, printed, edited and performed live, then recorded, for release on CD and download; prompt and cue books finalised; and sound, lighting, automation, stage and audio-visual calls set and made. Scripts have been commissioned and developed. Our technical, production and stage management teams have brought everything together through rehearsals and into performance.

Our actors and performers, engaged through our casting department, are always supported and kept in top form by company managers, chaperones, voice, text and movement specialists, whether at home or on tour. The logistical planning and implementation behind our tours is genuinely awe-inspiring: from our First Encounter tours visiting schools and community venues, through national tours like *A Midsummer Night's Dream*, to the international *King & Country* tour, which in 2016 visited China and the USA. Producers, production managers and their teams work to the finest level of detail in order to maintain the consistent quality and safety of RSC productions wherever we perform, for every audience member.

All of this is so that we can share our work with wider audiences, whether they be visitors, participants, ticket purchasers, cinema viewers, online communities, tea drinkers, cake eaters, Members, Patrons – everyone who comes into contact with the RSC in any way. Marketing and sales teams work to spread the word about our activities (including designing all our advertising materials and theatre programmes in-house, whether print or online). They set up theatre-seating maps to help issue tickets accurately and quickly (our Box Office team have an encyclopaedic knowledge of our productions and theatres) and to meet any specific requirements audience members may have. We talk to our existing audiences and to those who have yet to attend, gaining insight to make sure that we meet everyone's needs and provide the best welcome for all. Press and communications activity ensures coverage of our work, providing stories and great images, generating interest and engaging in conversations so that we talk to as many different people as possible. Without this relationship with our audiences, our work is for nothing. We are for everyone and do all we can to share that message.

Our teams strive to make every visit to the RSC a special one. Many different activities take place front of house – guiding tours, ticketing, ushering, selling ice creams and programmes, serving customers in the shop, bars, cafe and restaurant – and everyone works together to ensure the enjoyment, comfort, safety and security of our visitors. All of our food is prepared and cooked on site, whether catering for our public cafes and restaurant, our backstage Green Room, or events such as weddings and parties. Our retail warehouse is always busy, fulfilling online orders and keeping the shop stocked with items designed especially for the RSC.

This huge amount of activity helps generate the income necessary to deliver our work. We are enormously grateful to everyone who spends money with us, who donates, sponsors and funds us, and we aim to make those relationships enjoyable and rewarding. Our Development team are constantly focused on making sure that we fundraise, incurring as little cost as possible, to deliver our charitable objectives. *Matilda The Musical* would not have been created without Arts Council England investment. And its subsequent success was only achieved thanks to anonymous philanthropic underwriting of the transfer into the West End. The *King & Country* tour was supported by UK government funding, corporate sponsorship and individual philanthropy, as well as fees from US and Chinese venues. Similarly, we are pleased to share our many spaces for private hires: glorious weddings (on our stages, in the tower), proposals, corporate training events and trade shows, among other activities.

At the RSC, we have a 365-day operation (to be precise, 366 for 2016), 24 hours a day. Security team members are always on site and overnight cleaning staff keep everything in order. We work hard to recycle as much as we can, to reduce our electricity consumption (generating our own through solar panels on the roof of The Other Place) and to maintain our buildings. Engineers, facilities staff, property specialists, porters and internal help-desk operators are all part of the Company. They, along with our theatre operations teams, make sure that we have the correct licences, planning permissions, provision for emergencies, and they run complicated construction projects. Our information technology infrastructure is wide-ranging and reaches every part of our estate (over 70 buildings, from tiny cottages through workshops and our top-rated nursery to the theatres themselves – not forgetting our London rehearsal rooms and offices). Which reminds me, I never expected to be having conversations about booking satellites – at least two are required for each of our Live From Stratford-upon-Avon screenings.

Considering all this, it should be no surprise that the RSC employs well over 1,000 people. The 23 April birthday celebrations saw our peak activity, with more than 500 people working on site for that special occasion. Making sure that everyone is looked after in terms of support, training and development, occupational healthcare, contracts, payments and ongoing recruitment is the work of the crucial human resources and finance specialists. Paying the bills, managing our finances, complying with regulations: these activities might be invisible to the wider organisation but, without them, we would certainly grind to a halt. The same applies to administration and planning: arranging meetings, managing diaries, booking travel, devising rotas, answering phones, responding to queries and coping with the unexpected.

All of this is a long-winded way of acknowledging the wonderful people who make up the RSC. We try to work with respect for each other and for everyone with whom we come into contact. We are serious about our work and always strive for integrity. We enjoy what we do; we believe in what we do; and we love to share it. We look forward to welcoming you to the RSC again soon. Thank you.

Catherine Mallyon, Executive Director

2016 found the RSC absolutely at the top of its game; playing for the nation, performing across the world. We set ourselves the task of leading the worldwide commemorations of Shakespeare's death by reaching the widest audience that we possibly could. This book chronicles a Company that began the year with an ambitious tour to China in *King & Country* and ended with the most technologically advanced production of *The Tempest* attempted to date: Shakespeare's last play, reconstructed by our Artistic Director with the wizardry intelligence of Intel and Imaginarium, and a peerless performance from Simon Russell Beale, back home in Stratford-upon-Avon after 20 years.

We travelled to Blackpool, Bradford and Beijing, and opened a spectacular new The Other Place studio theatre in Stratford that remains utterly empathetic with the radical mischief propagated by its founder, Buzz Goodbody. Just as she did, we want everyone to come and experience the RSC's offering. The birthday weekend in April saw our President, Prince Charles, lead from the front in outshining eight other contending Hamlets live on the BBC. We are grateful to him not only for demonstrating measured delivery on camera but also for the unstinting commitment and enthusiasm that he brings to our organisation.

On the wall behind the bar in the new The Other Place is Susie's neon signature. Even more than the plaque in the entrance foyer, that sign speaks of the extraordinary contribution that Lady Sainsbury has made to our very heart and fabric. There was never going to be a good time for her to step down as Deputy Chairman but 2016 saw her do it in style. We can never thank her enough. Sincere appreciation also to my Board and Governor colleagues, to RSC America, along with all our donors, sponsors and members for their guidance, direction and support.

Finally, demonstrating both the fragility and the legacy of great achievement came the sad recent news of the passing away of our previous Chairman, Sir Christopher Bland. We owe him much and will work on in his memory.

Nigel Hugill, Chairman

David Tennant

KING & COUNTRY

SHAKESPEARE'S GREAT CYCLE OF KINGS
RICHARD II • HENRY IV PARTS I AND II • HENRY V

LONDON
BEIJING, SHANGHAI, HONG KONG
NEW YORK

In 2016 the RSC toured the *King & Country* cycle to London, China and the United States.

Griselda Yorke, Producer

On 18 February 2016, the curtain went up on the Chinese premiere of Shakespeare's *Henry IV Part I*. After years of preparation, the RSC's first ever major tour to the People's Republic of China, supported by the UK Government and J.P. Morgan, was underway.

I had joined the RSC six months earlier, in time to enjoy the launch of Shakespeare's great jubilee year with the Barbican's presentation of four full cycles of his second tetralogy of History plays, under the title *King & Country*. The cycle included *Henry V*, with Alex Hassell as the young King, which transferred from Stratford; the 2014 productions of *Henry IV Parts I and II* revived; and David Tennant's return to play the title role in *Richard II*, having played the part in Gregory Doran's first production as Artistic Director in October 2013.

As our sold-out London run drew to a close, the final t's were being crossed and i's dotted on the reams of customs paperwork that had to be completed to ensure the safe arrival of 59 tonnes of scenery, props, sound and electric equipment, along with hundreds of costumes and wigs. Visas and endless travel itineraries for a team of 72 (actors, musicians, technicians, stage managers and those of us working further behind the scenes) had taken months to pull together. Finally, here we were performing the Henriad (*Henry IV Parts I and II, and Henry V*) at the National Centre for the Performing Arts, better known as 'the Egg', adjacent to Tiananmen Square in Beijing. As Oliver Ford Davies wrote in a piece for the *Guardian* at the time:

> 'As I'm not in Henry IV Part I, I sit in the audience and find myself appraising this very familiar play afresh. It suddenly seems strange and daring. It starts with rebel warlords opposing the King (very Chinese), and then Falstaff (Antony Sher), this figure of anarchy and vice, takes over what had set out to be a history chronicle… We have been told that the audience might talk, phone, film and eat, but in fact they are silent and intent. There is much applause and cheering. We seem to be a success.'

Alongside the sold-out performances, Jacqui O'Hanlon, Director of Education, spent a day passing on the extraordinary work of the RSC Education department to a group of Chinese practitioners embarking, for the first time, on establishing education teams within their theatres. Gregory Doran led a workshop on Shakespeare with some of our RSC actors working alongside Chinese actors. Shihui Weng, our Shakespeare Translation Project Manager, organised a symposium on translating Shakespeare with many eminent Chinese Shakespeare scholars and theatre practitioners.

In snatched moments outside of the theatre, some of us were lucky enough to tour the Forbidden City, attend a reception for the RSC hosted by the British Ambassador to China, Dame Barbara Woodward, and even visit the Great Wall of China.

Next stop, the Shanghai Grand Theatre, where our indefatigable technical crew retained their sense of humour as, at one point, it began to rain in the wings. But the theatre team and audiences were determined to give us a warm welcome. They treated us to a visit to the Kunqu Opera Company, who performed an extract of the traditional opera, *The Peony Pavilion*, before teaching some of our actors the techniques and skills involved.

Twelve performances at the Hong Kong Arts Festival marked the end of our tour of China. Leigh Quinn captured the moment in her blog for What'sOnStage:

> '*We have hiked the Great Wall in Beijing, climbed the dizzying heights of the Shanghai Bottleneck Tower and now we find ourselves in Hong Kong, the King & Country tour's final stop in China. It has been an epic journey and we have met so many beautiful people along the way – hardworking dressers, quick-thinking translators, confused taxi drivers, t'ai chi gurus, overworked crew and selfie-loving audience members.*'

After a brief touchdown in the UK, we headed the other way around the globe, this time rejoined by *Richard II*, for a six-week residency with our partners at the Brooklyn Academy of Music (BAM) in New York. The RSC first performed in the Harvey Theater, then called the Majestic, in 1971 with Peter Brook's seminal staging of *A Midsummer Night's Dream*. It has been back many times since, most recently with Gregory Doran's production of *Julius Caesar* in 2013.

By the end of the run at BAM, five actors in the Company had performed in every single performance of the History plays since *Richard II* opened in 2013; a total of 515 shows.

I had only been around for a fraction of the journey but, as we collected in the foyer of the Harvey Theater, around one of the Folger Library's original quartos of *Richard II*, I felt a part of something very special.

Griselda Yorke, Producer

Antony Byrne,
Christopher Middleton,
Joshua Richards,
Sarah Parks,
Martin Bassindale

59,123kg	of equipment toured to China
72 members	of the RSC flown to China
4 goals	scored by Lyric Theatre Hong Kong Technicians soccer team against RSC All Stars
2 goals	scored by RSC All Stars against Lyric Theatre Hong Kong Technicians soccer team
104	number of times Henry V besieged Harfleur
1.45 miles	of fine ball chain toured to London, China and New York
732	costumes shipped to New York
10	prosthetic noses
8	prosthetic eye bags
7	moustaches
2	fat suits
1	fake roast chicken
47	swords
1,514	miles driven between Beijing and Hong Kong via Shanghai
2	bicycles shipped to New York
19,389	miles flown by the acting company
45,153	miles flown by the Production Manager
2	tennis rackets used in *Henry V*
91	computer-controlled (moving) lights
12	wooden stools
2	coffins

'The overall achievement here – which includes one of the greatest performances I've ever seen, Antony Sher's Falstaff – is nothing short of magnificent, a testament to the Company's welcome return to top form'

New York Times on the *King & Country* cycle

Ben Tyreman, Company Manager

When reflecting on our achievements with the *King & Country* project, the overriding sense is of its scale and ambition. As Company Manager, my responsibility was making sure a small army of 72 people (actors, musicians, technicians and crew) travelled safely halfway across the world to China, all the way back again and then off in the opposite direction for a six-week residency in New York. I also had to ensure everyone had comfortable accommodation on tour and that measures were in place to make their day-to-day existence as easy as possible. Of course, the key was in the planning. My own preparations began a year before our arrival in China and involved frequent communication with a range of Chinese colleagues at our partner venues. We were supported on the ground throughout these preparations and the actual tour by the wonderful China Tour Advisor Yangyang Tao, based in Beijing.

An advance recce to China in October 2015 was essential and enabled the small group to test-drive the accommodation and to experience the travel required between our venues. Theatre site visits allowed us to meet our Chinese colleagues face-to-face and get to know the layout of the venues in order to identify the challenges. A similar advance visit to New York happened during preparations for BAM. After returning from these visits, it was full steam ahead with visa applications for China, Hong Kong and New York, as well as finalising flights, accommodation and transfers for the tour.

I will take so many incredible memories with me from this trip… visiting the Great Wall, watching the sun rise over Beijing's Forbidden City and partying in the penthouse of Jardine House, once the tallest skyscraper in Hong Kong. In New York, our closing night at the renowned River Café underneath the Brooklyn Bridge was a treat… and the night Bette Midler came backstage was pretty special, too!

Ben Tyreman, Company Manager

Ben with Bette Midler

J.P. Morgan was the Global Tour Premier Partner for *King & Country: Shakespeare's Great Cycle of Kings* international tour.

The Royal Shakespeare Company in America was presented in collaboration with The Ohio State University.

***Henry V* was generously supported by Mark Pigott KBE.**

THE OHIO STATE UNIVERSITY

Global Tour Premier Partner

J.P.Morgan

THE COMPANY
DANIEL ABBOTT
MARTIN BASSINDALE
JASPER BRITTON
ANTONY BYRNE
SEAN CHAPMAN
OLIVER FORD DAVIES
NICHOLAS GERARD-MARTIN
ROBERT GILBERT
JULIAN GLOVER
ALEX HASSELL
JIM HOOPER
EMMA KING
JENNIFER KIRBY
JANE LAPOTAIRE
SAM MARKS
DALE MATHURIN
CHRISTOPHER MIDDLETON
EVELYN MILLER
MATTHEW NEEDHAM
KEITH OSBORN
SARAH PARKS
LEIGH QUINN
JOSHUA RICHARDS
ANTONY SHER
DAVID TENNANT
SIMON THORP
OBIOMA UGOALA
ANDREW WESTFIELD
SIMON YADOO
FISHER COSTELLO-ROSE
JAKE MEADS

CREATIVES
DIRECTOR
GREGORY DORAN

DESIGNER
STEPHEN BRIMSON LEWIS

LIGHTING DESIGNER
TIM MITCHELL

LIGHTING (CHINA) RECREATED BY
SIMON SPENCER

COMPOSER
PAUL ENGLISHBY

SOUND DESIGNER
MARTIN SLAVIN

MOVEMENT DIRECTOR
MICHAEL ASHCROFT

FIGHT DIRECTOR **TERRY KING**

COMPANY VOICE AND
TEXT WORK
KATE GODFREY

COMPANY VOICE WORK
AT THE BARBICAN
EMMA WOODVINE

COMPANY VOICE WORK
ON TOUR
ALISON BOMBER

ASSOCIATE DIRECTOR
OWEN HORSLEY

MUSIC DIRECTOR
GARETH ELLIS

CASTING DIRECTOR
HELENA PALMER

CHILDREN'S CASTING DIRECTOR
BARBARA ROBERTS

PRODUCTION MANAGER
SIMON ASH

COSTUME SUPERVISOR
STEPHANIE ARDITTI

ASSISTANT COSTUME
SUPERVISOR
SARAH HOLMES

COMPANY MANAGER
BEN TYREMAN

STAGE MANAGER
PATRICIA DAVENPORT

DEPUTY STAGE MANAGERS
KLARE ROGER
CHARLEY SARGANT

ASSISTANT STAGE MANAGERS
ANGELA GARRICK
LUCY TOPHAM

LEAD CHAPERONE
SABRINA HARRIS

PRODUCERS
KEVIN FITZMAURICE
GRISELDA YORKE

MUSICIANS
CHARLOTTE ASHLEY
ZANDS DUGGAN
GARETH ELLIS
IAN FOSTER
MAX GITTINGS
SAMANTHA NORMAN
HELENA RAEBURN
DARIO ROSSETTI-BONELL
ALEXANDRA SAUNDERS
CHRIS SEDDON
ANDREW STONE-FEWINGS
JAMES STRETTON
PHILL WARD
DEBS WHITE

Left: Alex Hassell

As well as the _King & Country_ tour, the RSC has been developing plans for new translations of Shakespeare's plays into Mandarin.

Shihui Weng, Shakespeare Translation Project Manager

The Folio Translation Project is a six-year endeavour to produce theatrically viable, actor-friendly and audience-accessible Chinese translations of Shakespeare's plays. A number of acclaimed experts have made notable attempts to translate the essence of Shakespeare into Chinese, but these versions are literal, literary and often overly academic in tone. The RSC's model is to embed the translation process in a rehearsal room, working with an ensemble of actors, and a director and playwright each from the UK and China. The foundation text of each play will be based on a new edit, created by RSC directors for each UK production, as we work progressively through the canon. Our aim is to link Chinese theatre makers and actors with translators and RSC creatives to observe their various approaches to Shakespearean text. Afterwards, the Chinese theatre makers and translators may mirror the process in China, under the direction of an RSC associate director or a Chinese director. Our hope is that this long-term project, developing individual play texts in turn, might ultimately reach a new folio edition of Chinese translations in time to celebrate the 400th anniversary of the publication of Shakespeare's First Folio in 2023.

Using this method, by the end of 2016 we had translated and staged _Henry V_ and _King Lear_ in China, and created versions of _Richard II_ and _Henry IV Part I_ and _Part II_ for use as subtitles for our Live From Stratford-upon-Avon cinema broadcasts in China. In 2017 we will continue the project, translating the four Roman plays and _Twelfth Night_.

Our first translation, and the first Chinese version of _Henry V_, was translated by So Kwok Wan, with input from renowned playwright Nick Yu Rongjun and scholar Zhang Chong. The translation was staged with Chinese actors at the Shanghai Dramatic Arts Centre from 11 to 27 November 2016, under the direction of Owen Horsley. A Chinese version of _King Lear,_ translated by the acclaimed Li Liuyi and Daniel S.P. Yang, directed by Li Liuyi, with the renowned Chinese actor Pu Cunxin [below] playing Lear, was performed at the National Centre for the Performing Arts in Beijing in January 2017.

Shihui Weng, Shakespeare Translation Project Manager

TWO TRADITIONS MEET

Pu Cunxin (who played King Lear in China) presented Antony Sher with a calligraphy scroll with the words of Gai Jiaotian, a great Peking Opera performer, describing the four great attributes of the actor: from striking looks or charisma, to emotional truth and the ability to inhabit the role with body and soul.

Above:
*Lan Haimeng
played Henry V
in Shanghai*

Chinese actors performed a new translation of *Henry V* in Shanghai.

Owen Horsley, Director of the Mandarin *Henry V* in Shanghai and Associate Director for the *King & Country* cycle

The challenge was clear. To create an actor-friendly, audience-accessible and performable Mandarin translation of *Henry V*, then mount a production in one of Shanghai's most prominent theatres with Chinese actors. Easy! As a director, these are the challenges that I love. The idea of sharing this play with a Chinese company and audience was irresistible.

Let's start at the beginning. The first day of rehearsals is a day I will remember forever. To give you a bit of context, the 16-strong company had been picked from a rep group of over 140 actors who are all permanently employed by the Shanghai Dramatic Arts Centre. We were entering their home and, at first, it felt like we were intruding. To them, the play seemed odd and distant. They knew Shakespeare was good but didn't understand how his works related to them. The challenge now seemed that little bit bigger.

As the rehearsals progressed, myself and Movement Director, Polly Bennett, adopted an ensemble way of working with the company, an approach that encourages the actors to feel equally responsible for telling the story and keeping the play alive and moving. There were a few breakthrough moments. One was when we taught the Chinese company a Scottish dance to explore the joy and release of the 'tavern world' of *Henry IV*. Suddenly the rebel Prince Hal came to life for them (and they all found a love for Scottish country dance!).

As we delved further into the rehearsal weeks, what I loved most was how *their* love for Shakespeare grew. Yes, *Henry V* was an obscure choice for them initially and, at first, the subject matter and translation were major obstacles to their understanding of the play. My solution was to move away from the academic idea of 'understanding' and get them to empathise with this young man who had been thrust into power, and to invest in his world that had, equally, been thrust into a period of war. As soon as they began to do this, the characters and situations didn't seem exclusively British. By week three, we were able to move away from the 'history' element of the play and to make it more contemporary. A fun moment in rehearsals was when we looked at the scene between the Welshman, Scotsman, Englishman and Irishman. Of course, this seemed impenetrable for a Chinese company. We decided the actors should approach the characters with dialects of China from their own childhoods. It connected *their* national history to Shakespeare's stereotypes and also stayed true to Shakespeare's intention of expressing the difficulty of communication during wartime.

The translation was another interesting journey. I had worked through translations in Spain and Italy but never in such a complex language as Mandarin. There were many challenges but also many joys and discoveries. I learned that every director should sit down with a translator and pick apart any play they plan to direct. I found myself more involved in this process than I thought I would be. The level of detail I was able to provide empowered the translation team by giving them a toolkit to hunt out the clues in Shakespeare's other plays.

This has been the most challenging directing experience of my life. Creating theatre is

 always thrilling but taken across different languages and cultures, it is truly special. This project was a reminder of the joy and simplicity of theatre and how Shakespeare, a very 'English' writer, can spread that joy in theatres worldwide.
Owen Horsley, Director

Ayesha Dharker,
Chu Omambala

A MIDSUMMER NIGHT'S DREAM

A PLAY FOR THE NATION

BY WILLIAM SHAKESPEARE

17 FEBRUARY TO 16 JULY
ROYAL SHAKESPEARE THEATRE
AND NATIONWIDE TOUR

In 2016, the RSC toured the country with a unique production of the nation's favourite Shakespeare play: _A Midsummer Night's Dream._ The professional company was joined on stage by amateur actors from local theatre groups and local schoolchildren.

Director Erica Whyman shares her memories of this _Play for the Nation._
'A most rare vision'

We started with a simple idea: to produce an enthralling and accessible version of _A Midsummer Night's Dream_ and to do it with 18 professional actors, five professional musicians, 84 amateur actors from around the United Kingdom from 14 different amateur companies, and 580 children and young people, plus a professional creative and production team. We wanted to celebrate the theatrical enthusiasm and talent of our nation and, by doing so, introduce many people to Shakespeare for the first time. I knew it was a terrific challenge, and a thrilling one, but I was in no sense prepared for the emotional highs and lows that were to come, nor for the way every one of us would treasure being part of this unique _Dream._

A wonderful team of practitioners – Associate Directors Kimberley Sykes and Sophie Ivatts, Movement Director Siân Williams, her deputy Polly Bennett, Voice and Text Coach Michael Corbidge, and Miles Tandy, Georgia Munnion, Sophie Hobson and Robin Belfield from the RSC Education team – joined me in travelling the country to prepare our amateur colleagues. We auditioned 586 amateur actors, invited 58 teachers and 14 amateur directors to Stratford for training weekends and we ran workshop sessions with amateur theatre companies. I also began a digital odyssey – setting the amateur groups tasks and giving them feedback via a bespoke digital platform that allowed everyone (when it worked!) access to my rehearsal room. It was like hosting a private version of the Eurovision Song Contest: 'Can Cornwall hear us?!', 'Bradford are on fine form tonight', 'It seems to be Christmas in Nottingham!'…

Meanwhile, we had to design the show so that it would be straightforward to tour and offer enough empty space so that all the different groups would be able to rehearse without any set. We wanted to create a world that had meaning for audiences now, but also reminded us of times when the nation had come together against the odds, indeed against a backdrop of austerity. We were inspired by the optimism and courage of the late 1940s, by trees – magical nature – growing through bombed buildings, and by the aspiration of the Festival of Britain to be genuinely festive and truly national. So Tom Piper created a theatre within the theatre, ravaged by war but with magic lurking in its bones. Titania's bower became a grand piano filled with romance and red roses, and Theseus and Hippolyta carried responsibility for making peace in their time.

'Are we all met?'

The most insane rehearsal process ever undertaken began. On Mondays and Fridays it resembled normality, working with just the professional team. On Tuesdays, Wednesdays and Thursdays, armed with a digital kit, Sophie, Kimberley and I would travel to a different amateur company each week, to broadcast from there and from the Clapham rehearsal room for the 'nation' to watch. These rehearsals had to be in the evening to accommodate our amateur colleagues' day jobs, so very long hours were worked by all. It took me several weeks to learn not to shout at the screen in order to command the attention of 102 actors. All of this was being captured by nine BBC documentary crews, who were making nine regional programmes about the amateur companies for *Inside Out*. It was entirely worth it though, for the moment The Bear Pit, one of our Stratford companies, joined us in Clapham to perform Pyramus and Thisbe and received a spontaneous standing ovation from the entire professional cast.

Suddenly we were in technical rehearsals in Stratford, with the other amateur groups watching via live link-up and teachers all over the country trying to keep up with changes to the children's scenes. And then it was on… national critics watching as we learned that every performance would, of course, be quite different. To our enormous relief, audiences were positively giddy at our mad enterprise! Before we had time to

catch our breath, we were in Newcastle to begin the tour and then the real joy and terror began, as we saw just what it meant to each and every participant who we'd invited to share our stage.

'With this field dew consecrate'

For our young fairies, aged between seven and 11, being asked to sing and speak in a professional production, to act alongside RSC actors, was often a dream come true. Just as often, it was a discovery that this was a place where they could shine, a place where we expected great things of them and where they could prove to the grown-ups in their lives that great things were no problem at all. The discipline, focus, intelligence and charm of these young people won our hearts every day and Shakespeare's words, so full of mystery and power, so beautifully understood by 580 very different children, were the passport to their confidence. Perhaps the most moving moments were when parents who hadn't set foot in a theatre before, who had not known what their children had been so busy rehearsing, finally saw what their daughters and sons had done, and beamed and, sometimes, wept with pride. ▶

Laura Harding, Sam Redford

A brief timeline of the project

2014

25 March	Theatre Partners' Day – representatives from the theatres on the tour come to Stratford to find out about the production.
3 September	The first announcement about *Dream* is made in the press and on social media.

2015

7 February – 7 June	Auditions are held every weekend with amateur groups nationwide.
27 February	Teacher Training Day – 58 teachers from the schools taking part gather to hear more.
24 June	On Midsummer Night, the RSC announces the 14 amateur groups chosen for the tour: The Nonentities Society, The Bear Pit Theatre Company, The People's Theatre, The Castle Players, The Citizens Dream Players, Poulton Drama, Leeds Arts Centre, The Canterbury Players, The Common Lot, Lovelace Theatre Group, Carnon Downs Drama Group, The Tower Theatre Company, Everyman Theatre and The Belvoir Players.
5 September	Amateur Directors' Day – each group is given a laptop for online rehearsals and to discuss the approach to the play with Erica. They finish the day workshopping scenes with the two Stratford amateur groups.
10 September	From their laptops across the country, amateur groups join Erica and the Associate Directors via digital link-up for the first of three tasks, designed to stretch and test the actors.
12 December	'Funny Men, Funny Women' workshop takes place with the amateur actors, led by Nick Haverson and Sally Phillips. RSC workshop leaders travel the UK exploring voice and movement with the amateur companies.

4 January	The first day of rehearsals. We start in London, take the company to Newcastle for a week and then, over the next six weeks, travel the nation, visiting the amateurs and directing their scenes via the digital link-up in the rehearsal room.
17 February	The first preview opens at the Royal Shakespeare Theatre.
16 March	*Dream* opens at Northern Stage in Newcastle.
22 March	The RSC's first integrated sign-interpreted performance of a Shakespeare play.
28 March – 4 June	*Dream* tours to Glasgow, Blackpool, Bradford, Canterbury, Norwich, Nottingham, Truro, London, Cardiff and Belfast. With a BBC crew at most venues, a turn on *Blue Peter* in Bradford and the directing and stage management teams travelling a week ahead to rehearse the children and amateurs, it's a busy but happy 12-week tour.
20 May	The BBC followed each of the amateur groups in the English regions from auditions, training and rehearsals to performance. They air nine documentaries: *The Best Bottoms in the Land.*
15 June – 16 July	Return to Stratford. Every two days another amateur group arrives to perform on the RST stage. Another 200 children perform in *Dream*. We run 72 technical rehearsals.
14 July	The RSC's first relaxed performance of Shakespeare starring 18 young people from Welcombe Hills School.
16 July	Final performance and last-night party! A huge celebration of *A Midsummer Night's Dream: A Play for the Nation.*

'Nothing can be amiss when simpleness and duty tender it'

It is impossible to capture the extraordinary journey of all our amateur colleagues in a handful of words, so they will have to forgive me for selecting a few of their number to tell our story. Every one of them showed courage, dedication and, at some point, leapt out of their comfort zone into pastures new and scary. From Andrew in County Durham, who, having lived through two kidney transplants, applied for and was accepted to the Central School of Speech and Drama while rehearsing for *Dream*; Maria in London who learned how to be kind to herself; Barry in Bradford and his enormous heart; Peter in Truro with his superhero shoulders; Lisa in Canterbury becoming the first woman ever to play Bottom for the RSC; Becky in Nottingham following fast in her footsteps with a killer impression of Les Dawson; Emma in Glasgow improvising a whole new dance sequence the night before we opened; to Alex from Kidderminster stepping in halfway through our first ever performance in Stratford so that Dominic could see his baby being born. These actors were heroes, holding down jobs as graphic designers, GPs, care workers, cafe managers, nurses, teachers, minicab drivers, pub landlords, then pouring their heart and soul into our play. Shakespeare carried them on his shoulders – with his deeply respectful portrayal of 'hard-handed' folk, people with real jobs as carpenters, weavers and bellows-menders, trying to put on a play and discovering all the hazards and all the joys of making theatre. And by their side, every week, in every region, with unmatched generosity and stamina, stood my professional cast. These actors were also heroes, investigating this most famous of plays with rigour and wit and soul and bringing it to new life, and doing it while opening their hearts to new colleagues and new audiences every day. We re-rehearsed the play with new members of the company 72 times!

'Your play needs no excuse'

What did we learn from making *Dream 16*? That this great, complex nation of ours is passionate about making and seeing theatre, and still knows how to come together to wonder at poetry, story and endeavour. That the poverty throughout this country is scandalous. That confidence has become a scarce resource because too many people don't know that they are valued, that they are capable, brave, generous and that their voice, their unique sound and viewpoint is vital and beautiful. That the pressures on our schools and our communities make participation in a project like *Dream* precious, necessary and urgent. That theatre, made with those communities and for those communities, can transform lives. We knew this last one, of course, but none of us had ever seen it proved quite so often in quite so many places. In Blackpool, where Anthony, Cathy, Huw (teachers all) and their team had performed to 700 people a night at the magnificent Grand Theatre, a town councillor got to his feet at our post-show discussion and said we had 'marked a turn in the town's fortunes'. It is a phrase worthy of Dickens, humbling to all of us, but it speaks of a nation that has allowed confidence and pride to belong to the few and not the many. Lastly, but perhaps most importantly, we learned that trust and respect is what makes the impossible possible. We treated every single member of the company with respect and we believed that they could do it – and so they did.

Erica Whyman, Deputy Artistic Director of the RSC and Director of
A Midsummer Night's Dream: A Play for the Nation

David Mears of
The Bear Pit

A Dream come true... memories from the tour

'Not many people can say they were cast by the RSC when they were 18. For a year, I rehearsed with a group of people who all became my second family. The cast and crew at the RSC were equally as special. I'll never forget how warm and welcoming they were, how willing they were to share stories, advice, laughter and love. These memories, the difficult warm-ups, the nerves, excitement, and pure elation of where I was and who I was with are things I'll keep close to my heart forever.'
Emma Tracey (Starveling), The Citizens Dream Players, Glasgow

'The tour often felt like a collection of city breaks and we always tried to experience something new in each location, from swimming in a quarry in Truro to completing a *Crystal Maze*-style escape room in Newcastle. It definitely felt like we embraced the quirks in each part of the country.'
Helen Fletcher, Assistant Stage Manager

'I admit I was nervous. Even in December 2015 (having been successfully cast in June), I still had no real confidence in my acting abilities. I voiced my concerns in an intimate and safe space. I told Erica and Sally [Phillips] that I was scared of not being very funny. Sally looked at me and said, 'But Becky – you are funny. You're perfect.' Erica nodded and reminded me that the RSC had cast me for a reason. And at that moment, I looked at my new friends and knew that it was all going to be just fine.'
Becky Morris (Bottom), The Lovelace Theatre Group, Nottingham

'My *Dream* experience affirmed my decision to make the huge change from enthusiastic amateur actor to committed professional – something I'd been thinking about for almost 20 years. I'm now studying an MA in Acting and pursuing my own dream. After this 'taster', I aim to return to the RSC stage as a professional in the near future. However, none of this would have been possible if one of my fellow actors from The Castle Players hadn't donated a kidney to me in 2014. I'd waited for a transplant for five years and this gift allowed me to be part of *Dream*. It made me realise how short and precious our lives are; they need to be lived the best we can and we need to follow our own dreams.'
Andrew Stainthorpe (Flute), The Castle Players, County Durham

'It never occurred to me when I first worked on the Bergomask dance choreography just how many times I would go on to teach it. From the first rehearsals with the professionals to what seemed like every primary school in the country, I must have danced that merry jig nearly 400 times over the tour.'
Polly Bennett, Deputy Movement Director

'The experience of learning the professional techniques used by the RSC has boosted my confidence as an actor. For my day job, I drive a minicab, which affords plenty of time to learn and recite lines as I drive around London.'
Peta Barker (Snug), The Tower Theatre Company, London

'Being in the advance party on tour felt like organising and preparing for the best surprise birthday party ever… every two weeks! It was my job to make sure everyone knew what they were doing and felt good doing it; from schoolchildren to venue managers, photographers to film crews, the locals to the out-of-towners.'
Kimberley Sykes, Associate Director

'Hand on heart, this project has been the most profound thing I've ever done in my 35-year career! I was part of the advance party, so I went to each location a week early. My job was to make sure all players relished the language and the storytelling with a passion and enjoyed sharing it across huge spaces. I always stayed until opening night and then pushed on to the next venue. And that was bittersweet – I would have loved to have stayed to see the show settle and develop, but I had to get ahead of the game and on to the next theatre…'
Michael Corbidge, Voice and Text Work

'The impact *Dream 16* has had on the whole school is already noticeable: attitudes towards Shakespeare have dramatically changed. Mentioning a Shakespearean performance now ignites palpable excitement. Recent auditions for *Julius Caesar* attracted interest from nearly 70 students; a remarkable number, given that we had initially struggled to get the required 30 for *Dream*. The experience has been life-changing for the students involved. Launceston will remember *Dream 16* for generations.'
Maddie Spink, Head of Drama at Launceston College, Cornwall, whose pupils played the Fairy Train

'My job was to recreate the lighting in each venue as the Lighting Designer had originally set it in Stratford. As we toured the country each week we would be in a different theatre with a completely different layout. Some stages were wider, narrower, deeper or shallower, meaning angles of lights overhead had to change. Slight differences in the shape and size of the stages meant we had to plan changes every week and adapt the show to suit that venue. It was always a race against time, as *Dream* had an unforgiving schedule. Luckily the team I had with me were super-supportive and we got into a great rhythm of working on tour.'
Claire Gerrens, Specialised Lighting Technician

Ayesha Dharker, who played Titania as part of the professional cast, recounts her _Dream_.

I met Erica Whyman at the rehearsal rooms in Clapham in October 2015. I remember leaving that meeting with a huge knot of longing – a feeling actors learn to dread. She was dazzling and inspiring; the project sounded bonkers and fantastic in equal measure. I was hooked. I geared myself up for the inevitable heartbreak of hearing that they had cast someone else. But then I saw an email in my inbox. I was playing Titania for the RSC!

And so _Dream 16_ began. Fuelled with adrenaline, we waded through three-page call sheets, Skype rehearsals with faraway Bottoms, and lightning-quick sessions with large groups of excited children, all held together by a team the like of which I had never seen before. The cast, at first bewildered, slowly came to trust one another and the crew; because at the heart of it all was Erica Whyman, showing us every day what it was like to pay attention to things as if nothing else mattered. Composer Sam Kenyon looked as if he had stepped out of a Quentin Blake drawing – a musical Willy Wonka. He and the Music Director Tarek Merchant would speak in a series of little nods and then spiky melodies would tumble out of the piano. Designer Tom Piper filled the room with spidery drawings and Escher-like stairs began to appear. Tech guys arrived and were just as you would imagine: quiet, ruthlessly efficient, terrifyingly young and cool as cucumbers.

Then the Bottoms arrived in London and I saw people who felt as I did. Thunderstruck to be there and determined, in spite of very real terror, to prove they could give it a go, because it was the chance of a lifetime. We did half scenes with each Bottom – never loading too much on to a first or second meeting. When I went up to one (I will not name him, but a mountain of a man), his hand shook like a leaf in mine. And when I had to fall asleep next to another (enormous, kind, talented) in the reinforced piano that was to be the bower, his heart hammered into my back. I had found my tribe.

> ' I am changed by what I saw and, in uncertain times, more inclined to hope '

Lucy Ellinson (Puck) made sure each member of the new cast had Puck-sized surprises (a Lion bar for Snug the lion, tiny almanacs for Quince, and so on). She would always wait in the wings and chat to the children before and after the show; let them try on her hat; work on their final speeches in the interval. I got used to seeing boys and girls look in awe at this magnificent androgynous person who they believed really was Puck: a proper Shakespearean superhero who wasn't afraid to show she was very human.

The children were the most _Dream_-ish of all. They plastered on their Holi colours like war paint and became brave. I will never forget one little boy from Newcastle, with his full cheeks and turned-up collar, encountering a theatre for the first time. The way he watched the argument between Oberon and Titania told me he had seen things beyond his years. He didn't smile for a day. Sitting in the auditorium, I watched the children as they filed on to the stage for the first time, as they looked into the dark seats that were to hold their families, possibly competitive friends, and strangers. I saw his face light up. He did not smile but just looked with a child's wonder at the space… So, when people ask how it all went, I say it went OK. I am changed by what I saw and felt and, in uncertain times, more inclined to hope.

Ayesha Dharker, Titania

A Midsummer Night's Dream: A Play for the Nation was supported by the Arts Council England Cross Border Touring Fund.

SHAKESPEARE'S BIRTHDAY

Shakespeare's birthday in 2016 was a tremendous celebration of Stratford's famous son.

With approximately 55,000 people visiting Stratford, the buzz on the streets of the town was palpable. The day began with the traditional parade, and after the flag unfurling and moments of commemoration, a New Orleans jazz band led the route down to Holy Trinity Church in jazz funeral style. At the Royal Shakespeare Theatre, while preparations for the evening's televised performance continued, we ran a range of free activities giving visitors an insight into theatre skills, stage make-up and our season's productions.

We wanted to create a moment of convergence, spectacle and excitement during the afternoon, so we commissioned one of the UK's finest aerial and physical theatre companies, Mimbre, to create a new outdoor show for the day, *Wondrous Strange*, to be performed in the Bancroft Gardens. Directed by Lina Johannsen and designed by Loren Elstein, the company of six performers took audiences on a whistle-stop tour through some of the most iconic moments and characters from Shakespeare's plays, often expanding on

Dramatic displays marked the finale of the birthday weekend

33

episodes that are just alluded to, and all represented through movement. Juliet balanced at the top of a ladder while a love-struck Romeo gazed up at her; Ophelia floated past on a bed of flower petals; and, at the denouement, all were chased off through the crowds, pursued by a bear. Presented twice over the course of the afternoon, it was seen by approximately 5,000 people, and also broadcast live on Periscope.

It was buzzing over at The Other Place, newly reopened and home for the weekend to BBC Radio 3, who broadcast music and performances inspired by Shakespeare under the title *Sounds of Shakespeare*. This residency saw Radio 3 take root at King Edward VI School, Holy Trinity Church and The Other Place. We hosted a pop-up studio in the foyer and this was accompanied by live performances on stage in the studio theatre. We welcomed thousands of visitors over this exciting three-day event.

All day we prepared for the finale, a spectacular fireworks display created by Emergency Exit Arts, with whom we first collaborated for the 450th anniversary of Shakespeare's birth in 2014. Watched by 10,000 people from the Bancroft Gardens and the opposite side of the Avon, and completed by an astonishing depiction of Shakespeare's face in flames, the display also provided a fitting backdrop as the credits rolled at the end of *Shakespeare Live!* The music for the display was played live by the Orchestra of the Swan inside the theatre, beginning with *Dance of the Knights* from Prokofiev's *Romeo and Juliet*, with the pyrotechnics perfectly timed to match the intensity and pulsating beats of the music. The display finished in a more romantic mood set against the *Love Theme* from Tchaikovsky's music for the same play. At its conclusion, you could just hear the muffled bells of Holy Trinity Church ringing to signify that the church was open for a candlelit vigil at Shakespeare's grave. Approximately 3,000 people then walked through the Avonbank Gardens to visit the church. The churchyard gates were lit with flaming torches, and the interior by 150 white candles. After the excitement of the day, we finished with a moment of quiet reflection, paying our respects to the writer and dramatist who has given us so much.

Louisa Davies, Events Manager

SHAKESPEARE LIVE!

On 23 April the Royal Shakespeare Theatre played host to a very special event, the defining celebration of the entire 400th-anniversary year: *Shakespeare Live! From the RSC*, broadcast live by the BBC. John Wyver, Director of Screen Productions, remembers the run up to this extraordinary event.

Shakespeare Live! began with a conversation between Gregory Doran and the BBC's Director General Tony Hall over two years before the anniversary. Among the ideas discussed was that together the RSC and the BBC would mount a celebration of Shakespeare and his influence on all the other art forms, from opera and ballet to jazz, musical theatre and rap, which would be broadcast live from the Royal Shakespeare Theatre (RST) in Stratford-upon-Avon on Saturday 23 April, the 400th anniversary of his death.

On Shakespeare's birthday in 2014 the RSC welcomed a coach party of BBC folk to Stratford to brainstorm ideas for what might be done two years hence. In August we started to discuss specifics with BBC Head of Events Phil Dolling, who became the project's Executive Producer and a much-valued collaborator, and he began to assemble a BBC team that eventually included Producer Catherine Stirk and Television Director Bridget Caldwell. Many of the camera, sound and technical crews on the night had worked with us on the Live From Stratford-upon-Avon cinema broadcasts, and established relations with the RST technical teams meant that things came together very efficiently.

At that point we hadn't agreed a title, and it often felt as if this occupied more discussion for over a year than any other aspect of the project. *The Shakespeare Spectacular. The Shakespeare Show. Strictly Shakespeare.* But once we settled on *Shakespeare Live From the RSC* everyone began to come round.

From the beginning, RSC Head of Music Bruce O'Neil and Greg were determined that we would have a full orchestra on stage – something that the theatre had never witnessed before. So, Bruce brought on board Orchestra of the Swan's 68 players to create a wonderfully rich and dense sound, supplemented by 44 members of the chorus of English National Opera and 10 principals for the climax of Verdi's *Falstaff*.

Early on, simply getting in touch with the enormous cast and creative team was a Herculean task and, throughout, we were hugely indebted to Greg's indefatigable assistant Jane Tassell for keeping everyone in touch, whether Greg was in Beijing or Brooklyn. Bringing everyone to Stratford for rehearsals and the performance, feeding and, in some cases, housing them, not to mention getting them on- and off-stage at the right time was taken on with great good humour and extraordinary efficiency by Assistant Producer Jake Bartle, Deputy Stage Manager George Hims and, the true heroine of the night, Stage Manager Linda Fitzpatrick.

A galaxy of stars joined us for Shakespeare Live!

By the late summer of 2015 the unflappable Stage Producer Hedda Beeby was on board, and she started the serious business of pinning down the promises of participation made by actors and singers in response to Greg's initial approaches. Co-host David Tennant was one of the first to be confirmed, even if we had to rework the schedule of his appearances in *Richard II* at BAM [Brooklyn Academy of Music] to permit him to fly back to Britain in the last week and return to New York for two final performances after the show.

Designer Rob Jones, who worked with Greg on *Hamlet* in 2008-9, started to conjure up the visual magic of a set with a video proscenium, a shiny floor, a retractable 'tongue' and three levels for Orchestra of the Swan – all of which looked just glorious on screen on the night. And then it became an organised and structured scramble from the beginning of the year, with endless rounds of recces and rehearsals, meetings about budgets, parking, security and social media, as well as thrilling confirmations and one or two reluctant withdrawals.

With just over a week to go, starting on Saturday night, our production of *Hamlet* was derigged from the theatre and our stage and set began to go in. The BBC's trucks and cameras arrived on Wednesday and rehearsals began in earnest on Thursday – although what was called 'A line of Hamlets' was only run with all of its participants for the first time on Saturday at 5.30pm (after we had done a dress run at 1.30pm, when we all saw something of what we had created from end-to-end for the first time).

Even in the dress rehearsal we had Assistant Director Josh Roche walk on with a 'Benedict Cumberbatch' sign round his neck, since filming commitments meant that our distinguished contributor could not arrive until later in the afternoon. Just the sign alone prompted an excited laugh from the friends and family of the RSC who had been invited to witness this initial run. Also absent, and played in the run-through by Greg himself, was Prince Charles, whose participation had been a well-kept secret for a number of months. Greg had been determined that the show would contain surprises and 'A line of Hamlets' emphatically delivered on this.

A line of Hamlets

In the end we overran our two-hour timeslot by 24 minutes. However, BBC Two very kindly kept us on air as Helen Mirren's Prospero segued to the beautiful benediction from the end of *A Midsummer Night's Dream* (with everyone in the audience holding up a flickering electric candle) to a curtain call, then outside, to the firework finale mounted by Emergency Exit Arts. Within minutes, even as Prince Charles was being introduced to the cast and creatives backstage, and as photos and videos of his appearance were beginning to be beamed around the world, the theatre crew was starting to strip out the neon head, the shiny floor and the video screens so that the new production of *Cymbeline* could come in for its first previews in the coming week.

John Wyver, Director, Screen Productions

' *Shakespeare Live!* was an apt and vivid reminder of the playwright's chameleon brilliance, his astonishing powers of assimilation, and the way in which the inspired juxtapositions of his language and poetry can ignite the cortical synapses of the imagination like no one in our literature. As usual, the man himself, always so impossible to pin down, was strangely absent, being both there and not there. Which is only another way of saying that Shakespeare, at once timeless and universal, speaks for the world. **'**

Robert McCrum, *Observer*

***Shakespeare Live! From the RSC* was broadcast across America on PBS on 23 December.**

HAMLET

BY WILLIAM SHAKESPEARE

12 MARCH TO 13 AUGUST
ROYAL SHAKESPEARE THEATRE

' Simply a **terrific** *Hamlet*, a blazing new star standing at the heart of an **intelligent** and **engrossing** production '

Sunday Times

RSC board member Sandie Okoro on *Hamlet* and its profound impact.
Paapa Essiedu is the Hamlet not only for his generation, but for this century. As Hamlet says, 'the play's the thing', and this is the story of a family the world over.

The whole cast was a revelation and the Jamaican gravedigger was inspired. As Maximus Decimus Meridius said in *Gladiator*, 'Are you not entertained?' What is the theatre, but entertainment first and education second?

I cannot describe what it was like to see a majority black cast perform *Hamlet* on the main stage of the RSC. It filled me with pride and, for the first time, I felt part of something instead of wanting to be part of something.

By casting the production in this way it not only entertains but it educates, as you see the commonality between people rather than their differences. Paapa's Hamlet unites rather than divides and holds a mirror

Paapa Essiedu
Inset:
Tanya Moodie

41

up to society as it is now: not just white, male and upper class. The night I saw it, the largely white audience saw black characters they identified with. I could just tell by their reactions (with my Stasi-like ability to order a Coke and a packet of crisps at the same time as eavesdropping on interval chit-chat).

Hamlet was the good-looking, educated young black man that they all knew one day their granddaughters or grandsons would bring home and that they would welcome into the family. Claudius was the nasty, slimy relative we all have and don't want to be left alone in a room with.

This production has had a profound effect on me. I feel even more empowered than usual and I fear I may be more insufferable than ever in championing diversity and inclusion. For me, it was so much more than just another RSC production. It was about the things that inspire us. Inspiration is the ethereal fairy dust that fires the imagination, and imagination is the invisible wand of change.

This production of *Hamlet* was a downpour of fairy dust and when I saw it I got soaked! I am forever transformed.

Sandie Okoro, RSC board member

HAMLET **PAAPA ESSIEDU**
GERTRUDE **TANYA MOODIE**
CLAUDIUS **CLARENCE SMITH**
GHOST OF HAMLET'S FATHER
EWART JAMES WALTERS
POLONIUS **CYRIL NRI**
LAERTES **MARCUS GRIFFITHS**
OPHELIA **NATALIE SIMPSON**
HORATIO **HIRAN ABEYSEKERA**
ROSENCRANTZ **JAMES COONEY**
GUILDENSTERN **BETHAN CULLINANE**
MARCELLUS **THEO OGUNDIPE**
BARNARDO **KEVIN N GOLDING**
FRANCISCA **TEMI WILKEY**
PLAYER KING **KEVIN N GOLDING**
PLAYER QUEEN **DOREENE BLACKSTOCK**
LUCIANUS **THEO OGUNDIPE**
PLAYERS **MARIÈME DIOUF, TEMI WILKEY**
GRAVEDIGGER **EWART JAMES WALTERS**
GRAVEDIGGER'S ASSISTANT **TEMI WILKEY**
OSRIC **ROMAYNE ANDREWS**
PRIEST **KEVIN N GOLDING**
PROFESSOR OF WITTENBERG
BYRON MONDAHL
VOLTEMAND **EKE CHUKWU**
CORNELIA **MARIÈME DIOUF**
FORTINBRAS **THEO OGUNDIPE**
CAPTAIN **KEVIN N GOLDING**
SAILOR **ROMAYNE ANDREWS**
ENGLISH AMBASSADOR **BYRON MONDAHL**

CREATIVES
DIRECTOR **SIMON GODWIN**
DESIGNER **PAUL WILLS**
LIGHTING DESIGNER **PAUL ANDERSON**
COMPOSER **SOLA AKINGBOLA**
MUSIC ASSOCIATE **JON NICHOLLS**
SOUND DESIGNER **CHRISTOPHER SHUTT**
MOVEMENT DIRECTOR **MBULELO NDABENI**
FIGHT DIRECTOR **KEVIN McCURDY**
COMPANY VOICE AND TEXT WORK
KATE GODFREY
ASSISTANT DIRECTOR **ANNA GIRVAN**
ASSISTANT MOVEMENT DIRECTOR
SHELLEY MAXWELL
MUSIC DIRECTOR **BRUCE O'NEIL**
CASTING DIRECTOR **HANNAH MILLER**
PRODUCTION MANAGER **CARL ROOT**
COSTUME SUPERVISOR **LAURA HUNT**
COMPANY MANAGER **JONDON**
STAGE MANAGER **MAGGIE MACKAY**
DEPUTY STAGE MANAGER **GEORGE HIMS**
ASSISTANT STAGE MANAGER **HETTI CURTIS**
PRODUCER **ZOË DONEGAN**

MUSICIANS
WOODWIND/NYATITI/PERCUSSION
DIRK CAMPBELL
N'GONI/PERCUSSION **SIDIKI DEMBÉLÉ**
GUITAR **JOE ARCHER**
PERCUSSION/VOICE **SOLA AKINGBOLA**
PERCUSSION **JAMES JONES**
KEYBOARD **BRUCE O'NEIL**

Right:
Natalie Simpson
Left:
Kevin N Golding,
Doreene Blackstock

Professor Ewan Fernie on how *Hamlet* encourages an audience to think differently – and mischievously.

'Lord, we know what we are, but know not what we may be,' says Ophelia. And perhaps this is the key to a play that keeps opening life up to new possibilities. *Hamlet* wages war against cliché. It turns its own established genre of revenge tragedy inside out to the point that, in the end, even though Hamlet has duly killed Claudius, and so revenged his murdered father, we can no longer be sure we're really watching a revenge play at all. I mean, to what extent can Hamlet be considered a regular avenging hero, or even a regular guy? He effectively puts the kybosh on his own most royal prospects, and in the process he utterly removes himself from sex and sexuality. After an interlude of madcap clowning (his famous 'antic disposition'), he avenges his father's death in a strange state of self-sacrificing religious inspiration. His ultimate achievement is to completely eviscerate his family line, handing Denmark on a plate to its rival, Norway. And yet, Hamlet is the figure who, in Western culture, has become our tragic hero par excellence.

I propose that the play encourages audiences to think differently, and that Hamlet's opening words straightaway announce this. In the first ceremonious scene at court, King Claudius inclines graciously towards Denmark's Prince and croons, 'But now, my cousin Hamlet, and my son…' But Hamlet interrupts, 'A little more than kin and less than kind.' 'A little more than kin' because, by taking Father's place and marrying Mother, Uncle has come too close. And 'less than kind' because this violently yokes together persons who aren't, according to Hamlet, actually of the same *kind* at all. Later Hamlet will mordantly call Claudius 'dear mother'. And when his stepfather steps in to correct him – 'Thy loving father, Hamlet' – he will respond, 'Father and mother is man and wife, man and wife is one flesh, and so my mother.' His first words in the play should be considered fair warning that nothing further should be taken on trust: that all regular assumptions are open to question.

'I say we will have no more marriages!' That is an amazing and shocking thing to say in a play, any play, let alone such an old one; but the Prince of Denmark says it, and his tragedy is so familiar that sometimes we have to remind ourselves just how radical it is. But perhaps its radicalism is not finally vested in any determinable meaning, however shocking, but rather in the fact that it is *Hamlet,* above all plays, that refuses to mean any one single thing. Like the shape-shifting cloud with which its hero teases Polonius – it's like a camel but no… it's like a weasel; it is like a weasel but now it's like a whale! – this is a play that won't stay still.

Take its most famous speech – the most famous speech in all drama: 'To be, or not to be'. It's a straight question. But typically of this drama, Hamlet doesn't give a straight answer. Everything he says about 'the law's delay', 'the pangs of disprized love', 'the spurns that patient merit of the unworthy takes' in fact adds up to a clear choice 'not to be'. And yet, Hamlet doesn't choose to end all his pain and torment with his 'bare bodkin'. So he elects 'to be'? Well, yes, but only because of 'the dread of something after death'. The mere thought of more being is enough to put him off suicide. In the end, he chooses life by rejecting life twice. His choice to be, at a deeper level, represents a profound and confirmed preference for not being. But we will see this only if we give

Paapa Essiedu

'A **new star** is born'

Telegraph

up the hope of a straight answer and allow Hamlet to draw us into the complexities of the question instead.

Hamlet is a play that plays with life and death. It is also a play written in Protestant England where a ghost from Catholic Purgatory pleads with a son from Luther's Wittenberg to avenge his murder. And, as if that weren't confusing enough, the Act V god who inspires its belated resolution is characterised exclusively as a god of 'rashness', one who releases Hamlet's trigger-hand, rather than encouraging him to repent.

Tragedy, comedy, history, pastoral, pastoral-comical, historical-pastoral, tragical-historical, tragical-comical-historical-pastoral': we can't even rest in mocking Polonius, for in its 'scene individable' *Hamlet* itself is all the things he lists, and then some. In its sheer, unfixing energy, it truly is a 'poem unlimited', one that is always presenting alternative forms and meanings, and therefore enticing its audiences to think for themselves.

The whole point might be to move us beyond the expectation of any simple meaning. And perhaps we get a further steer on this when Hamlet says what the play-within-the-play means. He says, 'Marry, this is miching malicho.' It is, of course, a teasing evasion, one which hints at an exuberance and menace that will remain forever out of reach. But then Hamlet surprises Ophelia, and he surprises us, by glossing his own mysterious phrase more plainly. He says that it means 'mischief'.

Ewan Fernie is Professor at the Shakespeare Institute, University of Birmingham, where he co-directs the MA in Shakespeare and Creativity. He is the author of *The Demonic: Literature and Experience* and *Macbeth, Macbeth*, co-written with Simon Palfrey. His latest book is *Shakespeare for Freedom: Why the Plays Matter* published by Cambridge University Press.

CYMBELINE

BY WILLIAM SHAKESPEARE

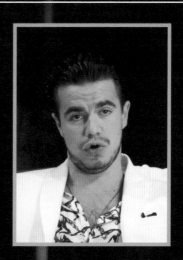

29 APRIL TO 15 OCTOBER
ROYAL SHAKESPEARE THEATRE
31 OCTOBER TO 17 DECEMBER
BARBICAN

**'Thrilling,
moving
and epic'**

WhatsOnStage.com

*Hiran Abeysekera,
Bethan Cullinane
Inset:
Oliver Johnstone*

**Assistant Director Guy Jones
talks to Director Melly Still,
Designer Anna Fleischle,
Composer Dave Price
and Movement Director
Emily Mytton.**

Why do *Cymbeline* in 2016?
Melly Still: It's a play about young
people coming of age in an adult
world that is struggling to make sense
of itself. It's in need of a resurrection.
In the play, Britain is undergoing a
kind of identity crisis. It doesn't know
whether to be part of a bigger empire,
or to assert its island status and let the
sea dictate its own independence.
That sounds like 2016 to me.
Anna Fleischle: The play was written
so long ago, yet we're dealing with
a similar struggle today. I'm from the
southern tip of Germany, with other
countries very close. It's bizarre that
you would not see that as a gift. It's
a misleading thought that in order

to be yourself you have to divide yourself from others.
MS: The identity crisis is happening on a personal and
national level. Everyone pins their hopes on Innogen and
the burden is too great; she must escape. She sheds layers
of herself, going from princess on a pedestal, to ordinary
woman, to servant boy in order to re-find herself.
And when Britain loses her, it loses itself and must
shed layers of corruption before it can be restored
and Innogen reveal herself.

Can you describe the world that you set your *Cymbeline* in?

MS: We created a dystopian Britain sometime in the not-too-distant future where the country's belligerent independence and insularity have taken root.

AF: It's a time when everything has dried up, and nature has been concreted over. Life hasn't got much of a chance, and the box around the tree trunk [left] exhibits the last remains. You can concrete over nature, but with just a crack of earth and a drop of water comes new life.

MS: The country has gone backwards – fuel is scarce and technology is a thing of the past. There is a flavour of the medieval and a resurgence of religiosity.

AF: Resources have run out. So we drew on the trend of 'up-cycling'. Rather than designing something from scratch, I created something with old pieces of clothing. Cymbeline's cloak is made from 100-year-old grain sacks; there's a corset made from the waistbands of jeans.

MS: Britain is decadent, decaying, litter-strewn and neglected, compared to the bright, fashion-conscious and multicultural Italy. We tried to communicate a sense of the wider European world by translating some dialogue into Italian and French, and Cymbeline's political machinations into Latin, riffing on Shakespeare's own irreverent blending of Roman and Renaissance worlds.

How have you been working with music in rehearsals?

Dave Price: I don't come with a ready-made scene, a character, or a place that needs to be represented through music; I watch the way a character moves, and the sound they make. The three countries have a strong musical flavour: the English scenes generally use Western classical instruments, whereas in Wales I've tried to create a sound world with a sense of otherness. Our Italy has more resources, so its music includes an electronic element.

Oliver Johnstone

How have you interpreted the 'dream'?

MS: The line that always feels significant to me is 'Innogen, I'll speak to thee in silence': Posthumus is burdened by his conscience, learns that repentance isn't enough to free him from himself, and that the only release is death.

Emily Mytton: In our interpretation, he loses consciousness and his unconscious takes over, conjuring up the family he's never known. It's as simple and human as that: he has to dig down into his roots. He then elevates himself to a god-like status in order to give himself the strength to heal.

What impact has casting a female Cymbeline had on the play?

EM: I didn't know the play when I came on board, so there's been little impact. It's more about the characters than their genders.

MS: *Cymbeline* explores the restoration of order from disorder. I was interested in shifting expectations by making both Cymbeline (the monarch) and Guiderius (the heir) women. Rather than the restoration of patrilineal order, it becomes about the possibility of a new order. Queen Cymbeline is no less flawed – she is still ineffectually trying to make an old system work under the influence of her devious spouse.

Arguably, the character most affected by the gender switch is Shakespeare's wicked stepmother – the Queen – who is now the Duke...

MS: I love wicked stepmothers in fairy tales. But *Cymbeline* is more than a fairy tale – it's a thriller, epic and mythic. Hopefully this interpretation of the Queen as the Duke allows us to focus on his actions rather than his type. It sharpens the audience's eyes to who he is: this is a man who is obsessively power hungry and loves his son beyond reason. Gillian (Bevan, who played Cymbeline) said that the Queen thinks she has married a homeopath, but has actually married a sociopath.

The characters ultimately move towards a scene of multiple reconciliations. Is it a hopeful play?

EM: Whether it's a hopeful play depends a lot on the last scene: how it's played and how the audience reads it.

DP: When I came out of writing the music for the battle, I realised that there had been so much horror on stage. By the final scene, it's a massive relief – it's cathartic.

AF: We don't know whether things are going to get better, but people see each other more. They've learned to look over their own borders – personal and national. The promise comes with the younger generation, who've been thrown from one side to another, and gone through foolishness to something clearer and wiser.

MS: Hopeful yes, but the play (not this production) is set in an epoch of great change, around the year of the birth of Christ. Shakespeare's audience would have known that what follows is thousands of years of war. So although the play's final scene is a deep gesture of peace and reconciliation, there's something in our guts reminding us that happy endings don't last. This ambiguity seems to be one of the key elements of a tragi-comedy.

Guy Jones, Assistant Director

Hiran Abeysekera

'Antony Sher is unbearably moving as the volatile king, in Gregory Doran's **stellar production**'
Guardian

Antony Sher,
Graham Turner
Inset:
Antony Sher

52

KING LEAR

BY WILLIAM SHAKESPEARE

20 AUGUST TO 15 OCTOBER
ROYAL SHAKESPEARE THEATRE
10 NOVEMBER TO 23 DECEMBER
BARBICAN

Andrew Graham-Dixon on representations of violence in art and theatre – and how we can't help but watch as this bleakest of plays unfolds.
Samuel Johnson said that he found *King Lear* almost unbearable. He was disturbed by the cruelty of the play, and by its unremitting bleakness – its ruthless insistence on a world in which there is precious little justice, and in which the only reward for virtue is suffering. All is awry from the beginning: Lear's first act is to make division of his kingdom, and family, in a disastrous miscalculation of love and loyalty. A 'wheel of fire' has been set in motion and everyone will be crushed or consumed by it. Nothing gets better – as Edgar later says, 'The worst is not, / So long as we can say "this is the worst".'

Those seeking parallels for the horror of *Lear* often look far beyond Shakespeare's own time, to 20th-century artists: Samuel Beckett, whose characters play out their own tragic endgames in wastelands every bit as barren as *Lear*'s heath; the Surrealists Luis Buñuel and Salvador Dalí, who subjected cinemagoers to the spectacle of a sliced eyeball; Francis Bacon, the creator of snarling, convulsed creatures – beings who seem like the collective fulfilment of Albany's prophetic vision of a world in which 'Humanity must perforce prey on itself, / Like monsters of the deep.'

Such resonances are hardly surprising. Neither is the fact that *Lear* speaks so deeply to the 21st-century mind. Shakespeare imagined a world gone mad, ruled by misguided or evil tyrants, in which justice fails and awful crimes are committed. Little wonder, then, that when we live in a world that feels so dangerously like that of *Lear*, we read the play so closely and borrow from it so freely.

However, it would be a mistake to regard *King Lear* as interesting primarily because it was ahead of its time. The revenge tragedies of Shakespeare's contemporaries, such as Webster, contain scenes nearly, if not quite, as bloodcurdling as the blinding of Gloucester. As an art historian, I am also intrigued by the similarities between Shakespeare and the wider world, particularly artists. Shakespeare was not just a writer but also a painter, albeit one who used words to create his pictures – so to place him in the context of art, as well as literature, can only be to understand him better.

Lear was completed in late 1605, not long after *Othello* and shortly before *Macbeth*. At almost exactly the same time, in Rome, a painter called Michelangelo Merisi da Caravaggio was creating some of the greatest paintings in the history of western art. He painted scenes from the lives of Christ, his apostles and saints, with an unflinching sense of realism. He depicted scenes of terrible violence that people could not bear to look at, but could not turn away from – a painter's equivalent to the scene of Gloucester's blinding. Take his *Crucifixion of St Peter*: a scene of torture, in which, sweating and heaving, Caravaggio's three executioners struggle to lift Peter into place. Just as Shakespeare dwells on the deeply unpleasant detail, so Caravaggio focuses on the deadly mechanics of murder, the roping and pulling involved, the sheer hard labour.

But where did it come from, this shared appetite not merely for representing the horrific but for embodying it with such repugnant physical and psychological realism? In art, this came from the Church. From the late 13th century onwards, it placed ever-greater emphasis on the human suffering of Christ. Artists were encouraged to depict the sweat, tears and gore of the Crucifixion, to place the horror of it all squarely before the eyes of every congregation. Caravaggio was the greatest heir to that tradition among the painters of the early 17th century.

Shakespeare, too, was heir to that same Renaissance tradition. Its imperatives were Shakespeare's: make it seem real, make it seem true, make your audience feel the horror of what you describe to the marrow of their bones. The great difference was that Shakespeare was creating his work within the new context of a secular theatre. Shakespeare, born in 1564, was a child of the Reformation's aftermath: a man living in the immediate wake of an astonishing cultural revolution, begun by Henry VIII and concluded under Elizabeth I, during the course of which virtually every work of art, save a handful of secular examples, had been annihilated; a man living in a country that had been deprived of its images and, in effect, been forbidden to see – a country that had been blinded.

Shakespeare's works would never have come into being had it not been for the Reformation, because without the Reformation the need for theatre would not have been felt in the way that it was in Elizabethan England. Theatre was the one, officially – royally – sanctioned art form within which it was possible to give people some form of visual spectacle, some form of visual imagining, as vivid as that supplied for so many centuries by the Church. Is it really a coincidence that the post-Reformation moment should have given birth to the most visually imaginative writer of all time?

King Lear is a play about blindness and sight. At its very heart is a scene – described by literary critic Frank Kermode as 'the most beautiful scene in all of Shakespeare' – in which a man, armed only with language, helps another man, who is blind, to see something that is not there. The blind Gloucester is led up an imaginary cliff to an imaginary height by

Above:
David Troughton
Previous page:
Oliver Johnstone

his disguised son, Edgar. Perhaps the scene conceals within itself an allegory of Shakespeare's own deepest vocation: that of using words to help England, blind England, see images once again.

Lear is like a whole series of religious paintings: scenes full of pathos and horror, like one martyrdom after another. Of course, Shakespeare could not easily have written plays explicitly based on the Bible. To do so would have been to face incurring the wrath of both Church and state which, in accord with the new tenets of the Protestant faith, strenuously discouraged all forms of religious art or any visual embodiment of religious legend.

Perhaps here lies the source of the discomfort this play arouses – the explanation for why Dr Johnson found it unbearable. The story is told in the bloody language, and according to narrative patterns, which would have been deeply familiar to its first audiences: the language of holy terror and of a Job-like suffering. But the story itself is divorced from any actual Christian context. There are no Christian altars in *King Lear*, no church structure to console us for the evils perpetrated in it – just a bare theatre, standing for a bare heath, in which a group of men and women enact a story from long before the birth of Christ.

Shakespeare, as is his way, gives us no real clue as to where he stands. He leaves us stranded on Lear's heath. We can impose our own optimism on the play, or find it utterly dark and hopeless. But he does not help us one way or the other. Does this world make sense, or are its horrors endless and without meaning? Make of it what you will.
Andrew Graham-Dixon is a leading art critic, writer and television presenter. He has presented *A History of British Art, Renaissance* and *Art of Eternity*.

BP £5 tickets for 16-25s and the BP 16-25 Shakespeare Pass are generously supported by BP.

Antony Sher,
Nia Gwynne,
Natalie Simpson,
Kelly Williams

57

'Faustus and Mephistophilis are **sharp-suited doppelgangers**, with Grierson and Ryan **burning a match** to determine who plays which role'

Sunday Times

DOCTOR FAUSTUS

BY CHRISTOPHER MARLOWE

4 FEBRUARY TO 4 AUGUST
SWAN THEATRE
7 SEPTEMBER TO 1 OCTOBER
BARBICAN

Assistant Director Josh Roche on the process of bringing *Doctor Faustus* to the stage.
Treadwell's is a small bookshop that sits right at the heart of London's 'magic walk' – a collection of spiritual and occult shops all gathered within a square mile near Bloomsbury. There are skulls and tarot cards in the window and thick books on the life and times of occultist Aleister Crowley within. The whole place is furnished in dark wood and there's a thinly worn cushion lying on a window seat at the back. As you would expect, the man behind the desk wears a black shirt under a black blazer, but is nonetheless eerily helpful. This is where I came across *The Book of Oberon* – a how-to guide for Elizabethan magic. This book, which is a compilation of different grimoires (spell books) from the 16th century, is stunningly practical. It contains summoning instructions on everything from the

Oliver Ryan, Sandy Grierson
Inset:
Amy Rockson

59

banal to the hellish – from curing toothaches and soothing headaches to conjuring Satan, Ascarriel, Annabath and Magrano. There is even, rather ambiguously, a 'Spell for Wednesday'. For me, this was the beginning of the rehearsal process for *Doctor Faustus*: sitting on the window seat of Treadwell's and reading through obstinately practical spells from 500 years ago.

A rehearsal process starts in a number of different places all at once. Months before, Naomi (Dawson, Designer) and Maria (Aberg, Director) had been compiling a web-based catalogue of different photographs, images and designs that formed the basis of an aesthetic style. Ayse (Tashkiran, Movement Director) and Orlando (Gough, Composer) had been in conversation with Maria about relevant actions, motives and tempos in each movement sequence, and Maria had been meeting and auditioning the cast.

Of course, the process then reaches a 'final beginning' on day one of our rehearsals and, like all creative projects, a blank page is a daunting thing. Maria had chosen to use our first week as workshop time, acting as a foundry for the raw materials we would later fashion into scenes, songs and movement sequences. The secret weapon in Maria's work is her clan of collaborators who are all equal elements in her direction. If you enjoy a topical metaphor (and I do) then you could say that the company of actors then act as conjurors under Maria's direction, drawing all the different strands of sound, movement and design together and harmonising them into something that makes sense, remains faithful to the play and is, hopefully, moving.

Oliver Ryan,
Sandy Grierson

There was, of course, something extra to consider in this process – the fact that actors Sandy Grierson and Oliver Ryan shared the roles of Faustus and Mephistophilis. Sharing a lead in this way was a new thing for everyone. It was a bizarre privilege to see two actors' interpretation of the same character develop in synchronicity and it was fascinating to see how clearly each actor influenced the other, as their ideas were allowed to cross-pollinate. Now that the production is fully completed, I can say one thing with certainty: you can be sure there would be no Faustus without Mephistophilis.
Josh Roche, Assistant Director

Above:
The company
Right:
Sandy Grierson
and the company

61

Composer Orlando Gough talks about bringing the hellish to life in his *Doctor Faustus* score.

What does the music of hell sound like? Britney Spears, suggested a friend of mine. Well, actually, not far off. The only time I ever went skiing, at a ferociously nasty little resort in New York State – one of the most hellish places I've ever been – I walked out onto the nursery slopes to find *(Hit Me) Baby One More Time* playing over the speaker system… and decided to give up skiing forever. (On the other hand, *Toxic*. Wonderful.)

We looked for a mixture of the seductive and the repulsive. Something that might promise more excitement than heaven – assuming you want the afterlife to be exciting – but is sleazy, brutal and frightening. Something that would kill you, if you weren't already dead. Something toxic.

The Elizabethans, mostly God-fearing people, had a rather different idea of hell, of course, but we're seeing it, at least partly, from a secular 21st-century viewpoint. The two most potent paradigms, in my mind, are the music of the great Tom Waits and the sound of an MRI scan. I have only had an MRI scan once and it was the most terrifying experience of my life, partly because of the extreme claustrophobia and partly because of the bizarre other-worldly sound – an assault of electronic rhythm that was all the weirder for having, presumably, some relationship with the contents of my brain. The lyrics of the hell-songs were constructed by anagrammatising the words of the Mass – a technique used in 'Black Masses'. This kind of cut-up technique was also a speciality of William Burroughs – a writer who seemed to have a particular insight into hell – and, come to think of it, David Bowie (which partially explains the elusiveness of the meaning of his songs).

And then there were the spells that project Faustus into this dark world. The lyrics came from the Kabbalah: an amazingly complex and – to me – almost completely incomprehensible attempt by Jewish intellectuals at a theory of everything, which formed the basis of Elizabethan

 attempts at magic. The music of these spells was based on a four-note figure which is both major and minor key – fittingly ambiguous.

Orlando Gough, Composer

Right: *Rosa Robson,
Ruth Everett,
Natey Jones,
Theo Fraser Steele,
Richard Leeming*

'A joyous piece
of popular theatre'
Michael Billington's top 10
theatre of 2016
Guardian

DON QUIXOTE

**FROM THE NOVEL BY
MIGUEL DE CERVANTES**

**ADAPTED BY
JAMES FENTON**

**25 FEBRUARY TO 21 MAY
SWAN THEATRE**

*David Threlfall
Inset:
Rufus Hound*

**Academic William Egginton
on the life and influence of
Miguel de Cervantes Saavedra.**
With a cunning worthy of a
Shakespearean or a Cervantine plot
twist, on 23 April we commemorated
the 400th anniversary of the nearly
simultaneous deaths of two of the
greatest writers of the European
tradition. Though neither Miguel de
Cervantes nor William Shakespeare
actually died on that day in 1616 –
the former likely died the day before
and was buried on the 23rd; the latter
succumbed some 10 days earlier, but
is dated as the 23rd because England
had not yet adopted the Gregorian
calendar we use now.

While the English-speaking world
especially reveres the genius of
Shakespeare, Miguel de Cervantes
shaped our world in ways that rival
even Shakespeare's influence.

With the two parts of *Don Quixote*,
published in 1605 and 1615

'David Threlfall as the Don, with his shaggy beard and **wild eyes,** even evoked Lear'

Guardian

respectively, Cervantes created one of the world's first international best-sellers; a novel that, in the words of the great critic Harold Bloom, 'contains within itself all the novels that have followed in its sublime wake'. But he did something even more profound as well: he captured in his writing an image of the world in a moment of wrenching, pivotal change – and he turned that changing world into a new style of writing that would go on to infiltrate virtually every aspect of modern life. Today we call that style 'fiction'.

As the literary historian Luiz Costa Lima has argued, prior to Cervantes' time, narratives were largely measured against one overriding standard: their proximity to truth. That truth was often a moral or theological one. While narratives did relate the deeds of men, a character who exhibited virtuousness or holiness would be written simply to serve as a good example to the reader. A character who distanced himself from goodness and piety would be worthy of a reader's censure.

Fiction is different. For a narrative to be fictional it must be written for a reader who knows it is untrue and yet suspends that judgment for a time. This double-edged relation to fiction allows the reader to engage with the characters he or she encounters in the story on a different, more personal level. Rather than see them from below, to be revered, or from above, to be ridiculed, the reader of fiction can step into their skins, can interact with the world through their eyes.

Today, we have come to expect the rich, insightful portrayal of characters in fiction in all of its forms, from novels to films to television series. But fiction's special ability to create characters that make us feel they are real, even when we know they are not, affects far more than how we entertain ourselves. The empathetic leap that is essential to understanding the kind of characters Cervantes created is at the core of the modern humanist vision of a cosmopolitan world of different cultures coexisting and accepting their differences. By developing a kind of writing that emphasised the common humanity of different peoples, Cervantes pointed out from the darkness of a stifling theocracy – government by divine guidance – a pluralistic future with religious, political, ethnic and racial diversity. Cervantes' future is one we can still aspire to today.

How did he do it? Cervantes' life was colourful to say the least. He was an impoverished soldier and exile; crippled in a religious war; kidnapped and held a slave in the dungeons

Below:
Theo Fraser Steele,
David Threlfall,
Rufus Hound,
Natey Jones

of northern Africa; freed after five long years and returned to his country only to be reduced to collecting taxes; imprisoned there on trumped-up charges; until, finally, he died in poverty despite publishing a treasure-trove of literary masterpieces in the last years of his life. How did this man create a form of writing that would have such a profound impact on all who would follow him?

Born in 1547 in a university town at the heart of what was then the world's most powerful empire, Cervantes' life spanned a period of enormous political and social change in the way European societies and their colonies evolved. Over that same period, Spain's sense of identity and worth as a people and a geopolitical power climbed to unprecedented heights, only to fall and shatter on the hard rocks of economic and political reality. Cervantes' life, from an impetuous youth devoted to war and adventure to the disappointments of his old age, seemed to cleave to Spain's own topsy-turvy fortunes.

Curiously, however, in Cervantes' case, a life of almost continuous failure forged unparalleled literary success, as the disillusionment he experienced at seeing his and his nation's aspirations deflated became the engine of his new-found style. By focusing his attention on how he and his fellows perceived and inevitably misperceived reality, he was led to imagine how the fellow humans whom he encountered along his wayward path both perceived and misperceived theirs.

The extraordinary dissonance between the picture his nation and church presented of reality, and the disappointments of his own experience of that reality, primed him to be unusually attuned to the suffering and misfortune of others. In a land where xenophobia was the rule, where estates were believed to be assigned by God, and where women

Gabriel Fleary,
Amy Rockson,
Ruth Everett,
Rosa Robson

were seen as naturally subservient to men, Cervantes created characters who explored the feelings and experiences of ethnic minorities, social outcasts and women. He not only described them from his own perspective but also learned how to imagine their perspectives and how they might be thinking and feeling. In his life he encountered people; in his writing he turned them into characters.

After a youth driven by nationalism, honour and war, a lifetime of defeat and humiliation wrought, not hatred and resentment, but understanding. This is the source of Cervantes' enduring influence on modern literature. For all its ribald comedy and social satire, *Don Quixote* is a book seeped in empathy for Cervantes' fellow humans, their ambitions, their desires and their failures. Neither staring in awe at figures larger than life nor satirising those less powerful, *Don Quixote* meshed ridicule with compassion, tempered the call of lofty ideals with a strong dose of realism, and in that way produced a fictional world so we could better see the truth of our own.

William Egginton is Professor in the Humanities at the John Hopkins University and author of *The Man Who Invented Fiction: Cervantes in the Modern World* (Bloomsbury, 2016).

CERVANTES AND SHAKESPEARE

The death of the greatest Spanish writer, Miguel de Cervantes Saavedra, is widely commemorated on 23 April 1616, the same date as William Shakespeare is generally assumed to have died. The same date, but not the same day, as the calendar of England did not coordinate with that of Spain and the rest of Catholic Europe.

Catholic Europe followed the Gregorian calendar (promulgated in 1582 by Pope Gregory XIII). But Protestant England refused to accept this 'papist' imposition and retained the old Julian calendar until 1752. Thus the two calendars were 10 days apart.

Nevertheless, the coincidence of the deaths of the two greatest writers of the English and Spanish languages in the same fortnight seemed to warrant marking. We decided to commission a new translation of Cervantes' greatest work, *Don Quixote*, to celebrate this anniversary.

'More than 400 years
after the play was written,
still **right on the money**'
Times

70

THE ALCHEMIST

BY BEN JONSON

26 MAY TO 6 AUGUST
SWAN THEATRE
2 SEPTEMBER TO 1 OCTOBER
BARBICAN

Playwright Stephen Jeffreys on Ben Jonson's brilliant and frenetic play.

While living in London in 1935, Samuel Beckett wrote to his friend Thomas McGreevy: 'They are doing *The Alchemist* at the Embassy next week and I hope to go. What an admirable dramatic unity of place the besieged house provides and how much Jonson makes of it.' Beckett, himself a master of the unity of place, is absolutely right: the house in Blackfriars, the setting for Jonson's play, becomes simultaneously a centre of operations for a trio of con artists – Face, Subtle and Dol – and a parade ground for the greed and folly of their prey. As the play goes on, the house itself becomes a character, surrounded by bizarre neighbours and possessed of mysterious rooms that we never see. It fully justifies Beckett's description of its 'feverish, obsidional atmosphere'.

Mark Lockyer, Ken Nwosu
Inset:
Siobhan McSweeney

Rosa Robson

But Jonson's handling of the other dramatic unities – time and action – is also worthy of note. The compression of the plot into a few hours piles more and more pressure on the fraudsters. Each successive set of visitors has reasons for returning to the house and, when they reappear, Face requires all his wit and invention to make their interaction profitable.

As to unity of action, there is a common motive of greed: everyone is on the make. Jonson intensifies the action with conflict, not only between the central cozening trio and their gulls, but also within each group of victims: Surly argues with his friend Sir Epicure Mammon over the efficacy of alchemy; Kastril upbraids his sister; the Anabaptists quarrel over doctrine.

Most notable is the destructive strife between the con artists themselves. Right from the start, Subtle complains that his share of the proceeds is insufficient, and when the wealthy Dame Pliant appears, the two men enter into negotiations behind Dol's back as to which one will win the widow (and her fortune). These carefully designed plots and subplots ensure that the action is moving relentlessly forward. Just as alchemy seeks to turn base metals into gold, so do the gulls and con artists entertain dreams of change. Wherever they are on the social scale they wish to be transmuted into something richer and more powerful.

The task of editing Jonson's play proved to be largely a matter of cutting. It is generally agreed that playing the full text counters against the speed and brilliance of the plot. When Jonson published the first folio of his works exactly 400 years ago, he seems to have made his plays longer, perhaps to ensure their status as 'serious' literature. In all, I cut almost 20 per cent of the play – over 4,000 words – to bring it down to a manageable length.

The other task was the writing of a new prologue. Jonson provides two: one, a clever acrostic (the first letter in each line forms the words The Alchemist) that gives away the plot; the other, a statement on comedy as a moral corrective. Neither is helpful in locating us in the play, which begins with a scene so furious there is a danger the audience will be left behind.

What is most striking about Jonson is that he wrote about the present – not just with *The Alchemist* but in other works. Shakespeare's Britain is all in the past – in the Histories, *King Lear* and *Macbeth*. *The Alchemist* is set in Blackfriars in 1610, the very time and place in which it was first performed. Perhaps this is why it strikes us as having a contemporary edge. **Stephen Jeffreys is an acclaimed playwright and screenwriter. He provided an original prologue and revised the script for this production of *The Alchemist*.**

Director Polly Findlay on the play's best trick.

For me, the most strikingly contemporary thing about *The Alchemist* is the way in which the play deconstructs itself. There is something astonishingly post-modern in its insistent, repeated collapsing of its own structures: over and again, Jonson invites the audience's confidence, only to pull the rug out from under their feet when he's most successfully got them looking the other way. His instinct for an audience's narrative assumptions leads to a masterful understanding of how to manipulate them: the set-up (three con artists take over an empty London house as a kind of swindlers' HQ) leads us to *assume* that the owner's return will lead to a moral reckoning for our protagonists – whereas it turns out to mark the point where the play changes its entire moral base system. Made ever more complicit with our three protagonists through every trick they pull off, we *assume* that they will see us through the action: in fact, two of them are summarily dispatched from the stage with hardly so much as an exit speech, while the third is gradually relegated to little more than an extra, almost irrelevant to a finale orchestrated by a character we had all assumed was a bit part. What beats Subtle, Face and Dol in the end is not so much an individual, but the structure of the play itself.

Ken Nwosu

CAST & CREATIVES

LOVEWIT **HYWEL MORGAN**
FACE **KEN NWOSU**
SUBTLE, THE 'ALCHEMIST' **MARK LOCKYER**
DOL COMMON **SIOBHAN McSWEENEY**
DAPPER **JOSHUA McCORD**
ABEL DRUGGER **RICHARD LEEMING**
SIR EPICURE MAMMON **IAN REDFORD**
SIR PERTINAX SURLY **TIM SAMUELS**
TRIBULATION WHOLESOME
TIMOTHY SPEYER
ANANIAS **JOHN CUMMINS**
KASTRIL **TOM McCALL**
DAME PLIANT **ROSA ROBSON**
NEIGHBOURS **WILL BLISS, RUTH EVERETT,
GABRIEL FLEARY, THEO FRASER STEELE,
NATEY JONES, ELEANOR WYLD**
OFFICERS **WILL BLISS, GABRIEL FLEARY,
NATEY JONES**
PARSON **THEO FRASER STEELE**

CREATIVES
DIRECTOR **POLLY FINDLAY**
DESIGNER **HELEN GODDARD**
LIGHTING DESIGNER **CHARLES BALFOUR**
COMPOSER **CORIN BUCKERIDGE**
SOUND DESIGNER **GREGORY CLARKE**
MOVEMENT DIRECTOR **CLIVE MENDUS**
FIGHT DIRECTOR **KATE WATERS**
COMPANY VOICE AND TEXT WORK
NIA LYNN
ASSISTANT DIRECTOR **JOSH ROCHE**
MUSIC DIRECTOR **JOHN WOOLF**
CASTING DIRECTORS **HELENA PALMER,
ANNELIE POWELL**
FOR THE LITERARY DEPARTMENT
RÉJANE COLLARD-WALKER
ORIGINAL PROLOGUE AND SCRIPT REVISIONS
STEPHEN JEFFREYS
PRODUCTION MANAGER **JANET GAUTREY**
COSTUME SUPERVISOR **SIAN HARRIS**
COMPANY MANAGER
MICHAEL DEMBOWICZ
STAGE MANAGER **SUZANNE BOURKE**
DEPUTY STAGE MANAGER **LORNA EARL**
ASSISTANT STAGE MANAGER **POLLY ROWE**
PRODUCER **KEVIN FITZMAURICE**

MUSICIANS
VIOLA/VIOLIN **KATHERINE LAMBETH**
GUITARS **NICK LEE**
DOUBLE BASS **DAVE STORER**
TRUMPET **STEVE LEE**
PERCUSSION **KEVIN WATERMAN**
KEYBOARDS **JOHN WOOLF**

Jonson's most virtuosic trick, of course, is deployed in his final flourish. He has already warned us openly that we are 'never more fair in the way to be cozened' than in watching a play; his closing lines bring us directly back not only to the fact that we are sitting in a theatre, but that the actor has, of course, been paid ('this pelf that I have got…') for the successful conclusion of the play's most epic con trick – the one that has been played on us. The audience is the victim of the play's ultimate sting, having paid good money for a fiction that disappears into a nothingness. None of Jonson's contemporaries, not even Shakespeare, were capable of creating a dramatic form that deliberately undermined itself in this way: it would be more than 300 years before most other writers tried.

There are no soaring Shakespearean metaphors in *The Alchemist*: Jonson's hard, glittering language ultimately points back in at itself rather than towards the epic or the divine and, in doing so, laughs at the very idea of the pursuit of a greater 'truth'. It is a play with venality in its bones, which regards identity as a commodity, and whose very structure points towards belief in a chaotic, morally unfounded universe, trading in pipe dreams and in which competition is the only god. As such, *The Alchemist* is a play that speaks directly to the culture of late capitalism – and seemed the perfect choice for production in 2016.
Polly Findlay, Director

Above:
Mark Lockyer
Right:
Siobhan McSweeney

'Polly Findlay's **dazzlingly clear,**
period-dress production'

Guardian

MIDSUMMER FAIRY PORTAL CAMP

19 TO 25 JUNE
AVONBANK GARDENS
STRATFORD-UPON-AVON

To mark midsummer, we collaborated with Slung Low Theatre Company for a week-long event and invited the fairies to come and join us...
A collaboration between the RSC and Slung Low, the Leeds-based theatre company that specialises in 'making adventures for audiences outside of conventional theatre spaces', might seem unlikely, but a conversation about what we could do together had been going on for some time. It found its focus in Gregory Doran's brief: to explore the Elizabethan beliefs associated with midsummer that provide the context for *A Midsummer Night's Dream*. In Shakespeare's time, Midsummer's Night was seen as being similar to Halloween, a time when the portal to the fairy realm opens and our worlds collide. People had superstitious beliefs that babies could be swapped for changelings, and blamed the failure of crops on the presence of puckish fairies. Interpreting Titania's 'forgeries of jealousy' speech from Act II Scene I of the play as a warning of climate change, Alan Lane, Artistic Director of Slung Low, proposed an artist encampment in the RSC's grounds, with all residents focused on the task of creating a ceremony to reopen the fairy portal, entice the fairies to join us, and re-establish the natural order of the world. It would be 'the definition of accessible, a place with no walls.'

The camp, located in the Avonbank Gardens, opened to the public on Monday 20 June. Designed by David Farley and imagined as a series of circles, its heart was a campfire, surrounded by tables and benches, and flanked by a wooden semi-circular stage, large tipi, kitchen yurt and herb garden. At the edge of the camp, nine bell tents provided accommodation for a group of just over 20 artists and crew. The design was a key ingredient in transforming the gardens into a place of community, creativity and generosity. Every day the camp served free food to visitors at lunch and dinner, and welcomed local people and children from Stratford's schools to experience the camp and participate in a range of activities. This included the entire first year of King Edward VI School – from the school building that Shakespeare himself would have attended – who took part in a mass ceilidh dance, and a small group of children with moderate learning difficulties from Welcombe Hills School, who enjoyed a relaxed sharing of songs and poems around the campfire.

The camp's residents included three members of School of Night, a group of actors who specialise in improvising in iambic pentameter, as well as physical theatre company RashDash, poet Nima Taleghani and a group of musicians – erstwhile Bellowhead guitarist Benji Kirkpatrick, singer Serena Manteghi, percussionist Tom Penn and pianist Becky Wilkie. A mechanical dolphin boat, inspired by another reference in *A Midsummer Night's Dream*, with opera singer Anikó Tóth performing on board, travelled up and down the Avon twice a day, and helped spread the word through the town about the project.

Left:
Fire artist
Erin Cunningham

Every evening we welcomed all comers to participate in the RashDash fairy rave: a mixture of silent disco and a dance class. It was followed by dinner and a cabaret-style performance given by the company. We were introduced to Herne the Hunter, the improvised stories of the School of Night, and songs including the anthem-like 'We are Blood', which became the musical theme of the week. Each night ended with everyone taking part in a ceilidh dance. All of the sound, for workshops and performances, was fed to the audience through Slung Low's trademark use of headphones.

The camp was timed to coincide with the return to Stratford of the *Dream 16* charabanc and we found opportunities for the two projects to intertwine. The company learned and performed the fairy lullaby from Act II Scene II of our production, as composed by Sam Kenyon. On the Thursday, Lucy Ellinson, in character as Puck, came and 'stole' the dolphin boat from the camp and took it for a spin down the Avon, chased by David Farley in the camp dinghy, much to the delight of passing locals and visitors. On the final Saturday, most of the professional company, along with Erica Whyman, members of The Bear Pit amateur theatre company and many of the Stratford schoolchildren who had performed in the production came to the camp for a flashmob rendition of the Bergomask dance, interspersed with sudden rain showers.

Later that day over 300 people, young and old, mostly from the local area, attended the project's culmination: the ceremony to open the fairy portal. The audience took their places around the campfire, making willow crowns as they watched the first half of the performance, which featured the best of the cabaret moments from across the week. During the interval a Gujarati feast was served by mobile caterers Manjit's Kitchen. As darkness came, the ceremony began. It was magical, otherworldly, yet wholly real and present. The audience and artists were co-conspirators in the final act, when Anikó became the Moon Goddess, and fire artist Erin Cunningham the Sun Goddess. RashDash performers were crowned. The portal was open.

> ' Generous, heart-opening, conversation-igniting theatre. The fire in our fairy hearts is well and truly lit '
>
> Audience member at Fairy Portal Camp

The following morning, as the tents were being taken down, a man on a bicycle visited the camp. He stopped in the centre, rang his bell, cleared his throat and delivered a speech: 'I just want to say that I have lived and taught in Stratford-upon-Avon for over 20 years, and in that time I have never witnessed such generosity. I live close by and have watched this camp grow from its small beginnings, I have seen you share everything with the people who have visited and I have been so moved by all of your dedication, work and creativity. So I wanted to say thank you.' And then he rode off.

With those words still ringing in our ears, we have been inspired to think differently about how we engage new audiences, and how we mark this important date in the future.

Louisa Davies, Events Manager

Fairy

THE OTHER PLACE

After a 12-month building project, the new The Other Place reopened in the spring.

The Other Place: a name to conjure with. It was first brought to life by the exceptional Buzz Goodbody in 1974. She was Resident Director at the RSC, and the first woman in the UK to be salaried as a director. She was a visionary: committed, heart and soul, to making Shakespeare live for everybody, and to finding radical new ways to make theatre and encourage new audiences into the Royal Shakespeare Company. Buzz's Other Place set the bar very high. Her *Hamlet* was praised for its 'vigour, essential humanity and contemporary resonance'[1]; and her politics were fierce, passionate and worn on her sleeve. Buzz died tragically young in 1975, having taken her own life. Forty years later, I am incredibly proud that we have once again breathed life into the whole idea of The Other Place, honouring her vision, while providing a new creative home for the Company, for visiting theatre artists, for scholars and for our audience.

The transformation of The Other Place was a recycling project on a grand scale: taking the magnificent and much-loved Courtyard Theatre (built to house productions while the Royal Shakespeare Theatre was transformed) and creating new, magnificent rehearsal spaces with views over the river, a new studio theatre (immensely flexible, intimate and full of character) and a tailor-made space for our 30,000 costume items. Now the company can rehearse on the Waterside campus, bringing actors and stage managers closer to audiences and the rest of the RSC team. Our costume store – continually in use as costumes are adapted for new productions – is more conveniently situated and, for the first time, open to the public on special Page to Stage tours that tell the story of a production from the first idea to the final rehearsal.

The new-look studio theatre opened its doors for the first time in July, with a festival of new work, *Making Mischief*, designed to capture the radical, provocative spirit of Buzz and the great theatre makers who, over the decades, made The Other Place so significant – Trevor Nunn, Howard Davies (who we so sadly lost), Katie Mitchell, Steven Pimlott and so many more – and, of course, the mischievous spirit of Shakespeare himself. The new plays we commissioned, *Fall of the Kingdom, Rise of the Foot Soldier* by Somalia Seaton and *Always Orange* by Fraser Grace, were bold, brave and complex; raising fascinating, often difficult questions about our world and the things we find hardest to say. They were joined by *Joanne*, a moving piece of collaborative writing commissioned and produced by Clean Break – a theatre company dedicated to telling the stories of women in and after prison. I revived Alice Birch's furious *Revolt. She Said. Revolt Again.* which joined the repertory before transferring to the Traverse in Edinburgh and Shoreditch Town Hall in London. The festival was a thrilling moment, attracting a very diverse and engaged audience to Stratford and igniting a charged buzz of debate and conversation.

Since then it has been a pleasure to see how well-used and loved the building has become in such a short time. Our founding partner, the University of Birmingham, has filled the spaces with students and researchers, making theatre alongside RSC artists and finding new ways to document it. The technical facilities meant we could rehearse the

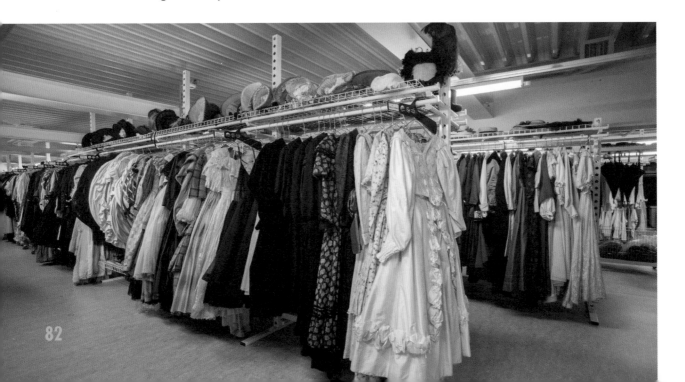

ambitious *Tempest* here, use the rehearsal spaces and studio theatre for corporate and community events, and use the meeting spaces for the Company.

The new Other Place, beautifully designed by Ian Ritchie Architects, with expert advice and ingenuity by Tom Piper (long-term RSC Associate) is a building that feels steeped in history and, at the same time, perfectly equipped for 21st-century theatre making. It is filled with unexpected light, and the deliciously welcoming foyer, created from The Courtyard foyer and the stage of the 1990s Other Place, is the heart of the building. It is a place where actors, designers, parents with babies and buggies, scholars, friends and strangers can meet and work. It is graced by Susie's cafe and bar, named for Lady Susie Sainsbury, whose generosity and bottomless commitment to the project and to the RSC made it possible for The Other Place to mean something for generations to come.

Erica Whyman, Deputy Artistic Director

[1] *Studio Shakespeare: The Royal Shakespeare Company at The Other Place* by Alycia Smith-Howard (2006)

The Other Place was generously supported using public funding by ARTS COUNCIL ENGLAND, and with grants from THE GATSBY CHARITABLE FOUNDATION, BACKSTAGE TRUST and J PAUL GETTY JR CHARITABLE TRUST.

Donna Banya

Commissioning the *Making Mischief* festival.

The commissioning of the plays for the opening festival of The Other Place was fast and deliberately provocative. In July 2015 we invited 14 theatre makers and writers to join us for a day and asked Reverend Giles Fraser, graphic novelist Darryl Cunningham and journalist Lucy Mangan to talk for an hour each, with the brief to tackle a subject that they thought was unsayable in the 21st century. Playwright Mark Ravenhill chaired the day's contentious debate. We then asked the writers to respond and, as a result, commissioned six new plays for The Other Place. One, Somalia Seaton's *Fall of the Kingdom, Rise of the Foot Soldier* was about racism and liberalism in Britain today: it was angry, provocative, beautiful and fitted the brief perfectly.

I met with other writers throughout the autumn of 2015 and, in a meeting with Fraser Grace, I learned he had written the first draft of a play about religious terrorism: *Always Orange.* I asked if I could read it and commissioned it immediately.

 The Other Place is a theatre that can and should explore big and radical ideas. Seaton's and Grace's plays captured a present, palpable threat to the fabric and stability of this country. This urgency was exactly what we were looking for.
Pippa Hill, Literary Manager

FALL OF THE KINGDOM, RISE OF THE FOOT SOLDIER

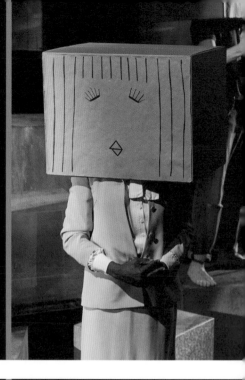

ALWAYS ORANGE

REVOLT. SHE SAID. REVOLT AGAIN.

JOANNE

87

'I used to hate English – as it is my second language, I found it hard.
Shakespeare has opened up my mind to think in very different ways.
I have developed a love of the language and a confidence to speak it'
Sahib, aged 10, Northampton

CHANGING LIVES AND ATTITUDES

TEN YEARS OF THE LEARNING AND PERFORMANCE NETWORK

Jacqui O'Hanlon, Director of Education
We were pleased to celebrate another special anniversary in 2016: the 10th birthday of the Learning and Performance Network (LPN), our national partnership programme with 11 regional theatres and 507 primary, secondary and special schools reaching over 690,000 children and young people.

The LPN was established to make sure that children and young people, particularly those with the least access to the work of the RSC, feel that Shakespeare belongs to them. Schools worked in partnership with the RSC and regional theatres over three years, participating in professional development, creative collaborations and performance festivals of work by young people. In July, to mark the LPN's birthday, we held a special event called 'Whose Culture?' to share the stories of transformation for children, young people, teachers and local communities as a result of our work with them. Here's what some of them said:

> 'Our pupils and their families have little experience of culture and performance. Exposing them to Shakespeare through the LPN has challenged parents' assumptions about Shakespeare and their aspirations for their children, as well as the frequent cycle of negative attitudes towards school and education. Parents have often commented that they didn't get Shakespeare, "but my little one now comes home reciting it and telling me what it means."'
> Teacher, The Canterbury Academy

> 'The children enjoy it so much; they punch the air when they go into a Shakespeare lesson. They are excited, something so often missing in schools.'
> Classroom teacher, primary school, North East region

> 'There is another life out there and I want to be part of it.'
> Parent comment following our work with their child at schools in Margate, Kent

> 'We knew it would work but didn't know how great the effect was going to be.'
> Head of English, secondary school, West Midlands region

> 'We define ourselves by our work with Shakespeare; we have staff applying to the school purely because of our work with Shakespeare.'
> Classroom teacher, primary school, Yorkshire and Humber region

> 'I am just so grateful we've done it; the single most amazing thing I've ever done. I can't really put it into words, it's ingrained into the way we teach.'
> Head of Media Studies/English teacher, secondary school, South West region

The Learning and Performance Network has been supported by Arts Council England, Paul Hamlyn Foundation, The Andrew Lloyd Webber Foundation, HDH Wills 1965 Charitable Trust, City of London Corporation, The Progress Foundation, The Ernest Cook Trust, Ian Ferguson, The Equitable Charitable Trust, Emily Hughes-Hallett Fund and The Grimmitt Trust.

100% of surveyed teachers reported that their skills, knowledge and confidence in teaching Shakespeare had been enhanced through the LPN.

100% of surveyed teachers stated that RSC approaches helped students understand the language of Shakespeare; students wanted to learn and to do more.

100% of surveyed teachers confirmed that use of RSC approaches had increased student confidence within the classroom.

Over **80%** of surveyed teachers reported that participation in the LPN had raised the school's profile within the local community.

DREAM TEAM 2016
Lizzie Hopley, actor, writer and Education Associate Practitioner

I spent some of this year working on a special anniversary project for schools called Dream Team 2016. The aim was to get schools 'doing', 'sharing' and 'making' Shakespeare's work in ways they never had before. Over 1,100 schools took part.

The education team produced a free Playmaking Pack for teachers that included 30- and 60-minute edits of *A Midsummer Night's Dream*, a specially commissioned musical score and guidance on how to approach designing and directing the play. Schools could choose to put on their own production, make Bottom's ears and wear them to school, turn their playground into an Athenian Wood, film students speaking lines or simply allow the fairies to take over their school (which one school did by putting fairy doors in skirting boards all around the school!).

In July, The Other Place and the Swan Theatre hosted a Playmaking Festival for participating schools all over the country; 1,500 pupils from 53 schools created 60 performances in a two-week Edinburgh-style festival of work, taking inspiration from steampunk, Prohibition and the refugee crisis. Groups ranged in size from just five students to 200. They came from all over the country, from County Durham to Newquay. Over 4,000 people saw the Playmaking Festival performances, including mums, dads and peers; 51 per cent of them had never been to the RSC before.

My job was to lead the workshops for those performing. I also had to work out how best to get reluctant children to perform in front of their peers, and to speak in 'weird' language. RSC practitioners are constantly developing tactics and games to encourage both of these skills. In the end, group after group of children – often in full costume and green face paint – confidently delivered lines of verse as if they'd discovered a secret language. They had become professional actors in miniature.

So often, it is the language of theatre, such as entrances, exits, 'on-' and 'off-stage', something we actors take for granted, that is daunting. The technicalities of character interaction before an audience can be problematic too. But the workshops helped overcome these difficulties. Once theatre is experienced first-hand, at whatever age, it never leaves you and, in this case, it had clearly worked its magic.

The transformative power of the Playmaking Festival was never more apparent than in the effect on its audience – one of which included a group of students with quite severe learning difficulties. Their facility to access the play's themes and iconic characters had been massively kickstarted by the fearless energy that a group of small children had shared with them. Theatre at its best spreads like magic from actor to audience. I have never led workshops quite like this before. One teacher's response sums it all up beautifully:

'Corby is a small town in Northants. Our school struggles, and big parts of the town experience economic deprivation. Sometimes it feels like the day-to-day running of school gets in the way of communicating our passion for English and certainly for Shakespeare… I'd like to share with you what one of our kids said on the way home. "I've got a geography trip tomorrow, but it won't be as good as today. Well, nothing will be as good as today, will it?" That was echoed by every student on the coach. Today, you helped 25 teens fall in love with Shakespeare. Life doesn't get any better than that.'
English teacher, secondary school, Corby

A DAY TO REMEMBER AT 10 DOWNING STREET
Leigh Wolmarans, Headteacher of Lings Primary School, Northampton
To celebrate the education work of the RSC, 35 students aged from five to 16 joined RSC actors to perform extracts from Shakespeare's plays in the amazing surroundings of the Number 10 garden. This was the first time that Shakespeare had ever been performed there, and the event included a welcome from the then Prime Minister, David Cameron, before students and actors performed excerpts from *Twelfth Night, Henry V, A Midsummer Night's Dream, Macbeth* and *Julius Caesar*. It was an inspirational, life-changing event, and one that our young people are going to remember for the rest of their lives. It was awe-inspiring to see students from our school performing opposite RSC actors in front of the Prime Minister. It defined what is possible for our students to achieve, many of whom are from very disadvantaged backgrounds.

Supported by
LLOYDS BANK

EXTENDING OUR REACH ACROSS THE UK AND AROUND THE WORLD
Justin Audibert, RSC Director

I worked on a collaboration between RSC Education and BBC Learning to stream the world's first live Shakespeare lessons for primary and secondary schoolchildren to classrooms across the UK. *Shakespeare Unplugged* (for primary schools) and *The Text Detectives* (for secondary schools) were 45-minute lessons, featuring RSC actors sharing the kind of work we do in a rehearsal room to bring a play to life. It was a nerve-wracking but brilliant live, televised event that was seen by over 30,000 young people and nominated for a Children's BAFTA.

The RSC Education department annually reaches

1,200 primary and secondary schools

530,000 children and young people

1,413 teachers

In 2016 the RSC produced an interactive game with BBC Learning, for children aged seven to 11, called *Which Shakespeare Character Are You?* The game introduces users to 37 characters, one from each of Shakespeare's plays. The RSC also worked with the British Council on a book for teachers called *Shakespeare Lives,* which explores themes that resonate with young people around the world today. It went to every primary and secondary school in the UK.

WORLD SHAKESPEARE CONGRESS CO-HOSTED BY THE RSC
Peter Holbrook, Chair of the International Shakespeare Association

In August, the RSC co-hosted the 10th World Shakespeare Congress in Stratford-upon-Avon and London. Along with the Shakespeare Birthplace Trust, the Shakespeare Institute at the University of Birmingham, King's College London and Shakespeare's Globe, the RSC welcomed 741 academics and enthusiasts from 48 different countries to the Congress. Gregory Doran gave the opening plenary session in the Royal Shakespeare Theatre, which included rarely seen footage of RSC past productions. The programme offered opportunities to engage with the current state of Shakespearean criticism, pedagogy, theatre history and performance studies. Over half of the delegates were attending for the first time; perhaps testament to the blend of sessions on offer. One delegate described the Congress as an 'intellectual laboratory', proving that Shakespeare studies are inexhaustible and continue to inspire ever-new approaches in the field.

CICELY BERRY

The RSC's founding Voice Director celebrated her 90ᵗʰ birthday.

'Cis' Berry is a bit of a legend. She has been intrinsically linked with the Company since 1970. She would probably scoff at the epithets 'legendary' and 'pioneer' but she really was blazing a trail; the job of voice coach in the rehearsal room didn't exist before Cicely invented it. She has spent her whole career inspiring actors, directors and voice practitioners, as well as a much wider community, from politicians and princes to the theatre company of the Brazilian favelas and prisoners from Dartmoor.

Cicely discovered the power of language as a small child; she had a passion for poetry even then. When she teaches, the focus of the work goes beyond the meaning of the phrase to the sound of words, their energy and rhythm – allowing them to resonate deeply in the body. This allows the speaker to truly *own* the words in a different way.

Gregory Doran, who first encountered Cicely in 1987 when he was an RSC actor, says:
'One of her favourite quotations is from Thomas Kyd's play The Spanish Tragedy: *"Where words prevail not, violence prevails." Cis' belief in the power of language is palpable in her work. It's political for her. It's physical. She connects language not just to actors' voices, but she gets it into their bodies. She releases imaginations and makes them connect with the imagery in Shakespeare's text, to need it, to make it vital, potent and alive.'*

Cicely, on her own career at the RSC:
'I have had a long and fruitful journey with the Company since Trevor Nunn invited me to join in 1970 – the RSC was the first theatre company anywhere to employ a full-time 'voice person'. Because Trevor wanted to have a mixed company – mixed in age, class and race – he understood that work would be needed to bring together and meld the way such a diverse company would hear and speak Shakespearean text.

'I have lived through many changes and developments at the RSC: one of the most important was the opening of The Other Place, and Buzz's [director, Buzz Goodbody] vision of how playing classical text in a small space would enrich both our understanding and our speaking of the text. I was also there at the opening of the Swan Theatre, and appreciate how that inclusive space can be used to involve the audience, and so arouse their interest and response to the play.

'Our priority as a Company is always to get our audience deeply involved in the story, and the moral and political questions it opens up. Shakespeare always presents us with an underlying moral and political dilemma. Shakespeare is always for now.'

Buhle Ngaba,
Denise Goldin,
David Viviers

BRETT GOLDIN BURSARY

The year 2016 marks a decade of the bursary that was set up to remember the young actor.

In 2006, young South African actor Brett Goldin and his friend, fashion designer Richard Bloom, were brutally murdered just days before he was due to leave for Stratford-upon-Avon to play Guildenstern in Janet Suzman's production of *Hamlet*, the play that launched our Complete Works Festival. The double murder sent shockwaves throughout South Africa and England.

The RSC, the Actors' Centre in Johannesburg and the Baxter Theatre Centre in Cape Town established a bursary to give other young South African actors the opportunity that Brett was denied, and to honour his memory in an appropriate manner.

In July we welcomed our final bursary winners, Buhle Ngaba and David Viviers. To commemorate Brett's legacy, we unveiled a plaque in his name in the Swan Theatre. We were all delighted that Brett's mother, Denise Goldin, was able to be with us to celebrate the opportunities that the bursary has given 11 young people, whose lives have genuinely been made better in her son's name.

Denise said, 'My family and I are deeply honoured that Brett's memory has been upheld with the incredible success of this bursary and it has been a joy to see how it has benefited the young actors who have been through the programme. Besides enhancing their own performances, these actors have brought back to South Africa their passion for Shakespeare and positively used this to encourage and inspire upcoming actors.'

Janet Suzman

THE TWO NOBLE KINSMEN

BY JOHN FLETCHER AND WILLIAM SHAKESPEARE

17 AUGUST TO 7 FEBRUARY 2017
SWAN THEATRE

Director Blanche McIntyre on approaching *Kinsmen* in 2016.
Being asked to direct *The Two Noble Kinsmen*, a play so rarely performed, was both an enormous privilege and an enormous responsibility. Any Shakespeare production has to speak across the centuries, but it feels particularly important to find common ground when *Kinsmen* gets out so little.
 It was a thrill to find out how contemporary the play is. Its story is about the way love can't be controlled or defined. Palamon and Arcite are too close: Arcite says, 'am not I / Part of your blood, part of your soul? You have told me / That I was Palamon, and you were Arcite…' It's not a sexual attraction, but they are the most important things in each other's lives, more than the woman they love.
 Other kinds of love include Emilia and Flavina (two eleven-year-old

'Blanche McIntyre's intelligent...
squirmingly funny production'

Sunday Times

James Corrigan,
Jamie Wilkes
Inset:
Frances McNamee

girls), Emilia and her waiting woman (the earliest lesbian chat-up scene I've come across), Theseus and Pirithous (whose 'knot of love' outdoes Theseus' feelings for his bride), the Jailer's Daughter (whose fantasy takes over her life) and her Wooer (who dresses up as his own rival to cure his fiancée's breakdown). This collection of non-traditional relationships is definitely unusual for the age, and it finds a parallel in a 2015 study of sexuality that showed half of British 18- to 24-year-olds identifying as non-binary. Another study showed half of millennials with comparable feelings about gender. Elsewhere, preparation for this production coincided with Donald Trump's victory in the US primaries, and a stream of news that showed a hardening of attitudes to gender, from 'sexist' children's clothes in supermarkets to Twitter-hounding of women in public life.

This was *Kinsmen*'s other subject – hyper-masculinity, and the problems you get when men are defined as 'pursuers' and women as 'prizes'. Palamon and Arcite's love for Emilia drives the plot: they've never spoken to her, but they're happy to kill each other for her, and their culture encourages it, not asking if Emilia has feelings of her own. Shakespeare and Fletcher's critique is constantly in the text, from Palamon and Arcite's flings with nameless women ('the Marshal's sister had her share too') to Theseus asking Emilia to choose a husband from two near-strangers (it's fine because they're both 'noble'). By contrast, Emilia and her sister are Amazons – intelligent, articulate ex-soldiers, who argue passionately against the system. The macho thinking within the

play is terrible for both the men and women. It's tragic for Arcite and Palamon, and all the men become diminished and ridiculous when they follow it. It's equally tragic for the women who are sidelined and silenced.

There is a class angle too, which came out in our costume design. All Athenians value material display, but the difference between the haves and have-nots is massive. The Jailer and his daughter are hard up ('something I may cast to you, not much', he says to his future son-in-law, and she has one petticoat 'and two coarse smocks') but Theseus, Pirithous and the Amazons can spend their time in endless leisure. Hence, all the costumes are modern, apart from the gods'. The higher up the social scale we went, the more we took inspiration from (often flamboyant) contemporary couture, while we looked for ordinary clothes for the characters who are just getting by.

These factors – class, gender and sexuality – mapped easily onto 2016. Yet there was another, more modern, element to the play. The script has three recurring images: horses, when it deals with a man's sex drive; the sea, when a character is emotionally overwhelmed; and woods, when someone breaks social rules or loses their bearings. These are so pivotal – including in the ending, where Arcite's horse fatally damages him – it felt like Shakespeare and Fletcher were anticipating Freud by a few centuries.

I decided to link this to the gods who decide the ending of the play. Elizabethan thought gave planets control of different bits of a person (Jupiter ruled the seat of emotions, the

The company

Above: Danusia Samal
Right: Allison McKenzie,
Chris Jack,
Gyuri Sarossy,
Frances McNamee

liver; Mercury, communication; Mars, a man's balls, and so on). By this, gods could be irresistible interior drives, as well as external powers.

If the gods are powers that work through people, love must surely be the greatest, as much now as then: an overwhelming force, beyond defining, which humans reduce to make it understandable and controllable. (This is probably why the men in the play, with their black-and-white thinking, are ridiculous and tragic rather than hateful.)

These elements came together in the Morris, our equivalent of *Midsummer's* Mechanicals' play. It's a sexed-up dance (it features a baboon with a 'long tool'), with a rigid hierarchy of characters from lord and lady to clown and beast. I discovered overlaps with mumming plays. These feature hobby horses, combats that lead to two fighters dying, and resurrections.

This felt like the world of *Kinsmen* in miniature. Like Quince and co, the Morris dancers present the other way the play could go. Pyramus and Thisbe is a lovers' escape gone wrong, the negative of the *Midsummer* adventures. In the Morris dance, love conquers all in a gender-bending, sexually fluid way, the social order is broken up, and horse-riding knights duel to the death but it still turns out OK. To bring this out, we nudged the dancers' cast list, so it burlesqued figures from *Kinsmen* (Theseus and the Queen), *A Midsummer Night's Dream* (Pyramus and Thisbe in drag), modern references (Dorothy and the Tin Man), and crossed the Morris music with Stravinsky's *Rite of Spring*.

In the play itself, of course, nobody gets to escape the system, whether they're men or women, gay or straight, ordinary or noble. There are no consoling answers and the ending is bleak. But the wish fulfilment in the Morris, and the questions that the play itself raises, create hope that, while we're on earth at least, there is the possibility of breaking down boundaries and working for something better.
Blanche McIntyre, Director

'A **carnival atmosphere** hits the RSC
as it celebrates the 30th birthday of the Swan'
Sunday Times

104

THE ROVER

BY APHRA BEHN

8 SEPTEMBER TO 11 FEBRUARY 2017
SWAN THEATRE

Director Loveday Ingram on the significance of time and place to Aphra Behn's writing – and how a carnival setting allowed the playwright to invert the status quo.

When I first discovered *The Rover* on a shelf in the office of RSC Director John Barton, whom I was assisting at the time, I immediately fell in love with this wild, mischievous play.

The action takes place over a short time period and is set in an exotic, foreign land during a carnival. Strong, witty women take men to task and, in most cases, get their way. I was shocked that I knew so little about Aphra Behn. As I explored her life, I was amazed to discover that she had more plays performed than her contemporary William Congreve, was a poet, translator and novelist, a friend of the King, was briefly a spy, and had lived a life that was so rock 'n' roll she became a byword for notorious, loose living. She was

The company
Inset: Joseph Millson

CAST & CREATIVES

WILLMORE, THE ROVER **JOSEPH MILLSON**
BELVILE **PATRICK ROBINSON**
FREDERICK **PATRICK KNOWLES**
BLUNT **LEANDER DEENY**
DON PEDRO **GYURI SAROSSY**
HELLENA **FAYE CASTELOW**
FLORINDA **FRANCES McNAMEE**
VALERIA **EMMA NOAKES**
CALLIS **SALLY BANKES**
DON ANTONIO **JAMIE WILKES**
STEPHANO **JOE ALLEN**
ANGELLICA BIANCA
ALEXANDRA GILBREATH
MORETTA **ALLISON McKENZIE**
ASTREA **DANUSIA SAMAL**
ADRIANA **LENA KAUR**
AMINTA **ELOISE SECKER**
PHILLIPPO **ASHLEY CAMPBELL**
BISKEY **LEON LOPEZ**
LUCETTA **KELLIE SHIRLEY**
SANCHO **CHRIS JACK**

CREATIVES
DIRECTOR **LOVEDAY INGRAM**
DESIGNER **LEZ BROTHERSTON**
LIGHTING DESIGNER **TIM LUTKIN**
COMPOSER **GRANT OLDING**
SOUND DESIGNER **FERGUS O'HARE**
MOVEMENT DIRECTOR
NICHOLA TREHERNE
FIGHT DIRECTOR **TERRY KING**
COMMEDIA CONSULTANT
MARCELLO MAGNI
COMPANY VOICE AND TEXT WORK
EDDA SHARPE
ASSISTANT DIRECTOR **ED VINEY**
ASSISTANT MOVEMENT DIRECTOR
TIM STANLEY
MUSIC DIRECTOR **KEVIN WATERMAN**
CASTING DIRECTOR **ANNELIE POWELL**
PRODUCTION MANAGER
DAVID TANQUERAY
COSTUME SUPERVISOR **IRENE BOHAN**
COMPANY MANAGER
MICHAEL DEMBOWICZ
STAGE MANAGER **AMY GRIFFIN**
DEPUTY STAGE MANAGER **GABS SANDERS**
ASSISTANT STAGE MANAGER
ALICE BARBER
PRODUCER **GRISELDA YORKE**

MUSICIANS
SAXOPHONE **ADAM CROSS**
GUITAR **NICK LEE/PHIL JAMES**
GUITAR/PERCUSSION **PHILL WARD**
DOUBLE BASS **MAT HEIGHWAY**
TRUMPET **ANDREW STONE-FEWINGS**
PERCUSSION **KEVIN WATERMAN**

pushed aside by later generations; her feminism and libertine behaviour too ahead of its time. I was passionate to redress the balance for this extraordinary woman and began work on the play.

The Rover, in its unedited version, is dense in places, the plot is confusing at times, but its heart is warm and its energy electric; it is absolutely of its time. Written in the 1670s but set in the Cromwellian 1650s, the exiled Royalists meet in a foreign land to search for love and to 'enjoy themselves a little'. Behn uses carnival as a vehicle to celebrate the values of the restored court of Charles II – sexual freedom, hedonism, luxury and easy gratification – and to juxtapose these against the despised repression of the defeated Puritans. Behn's nostalgic nod to the bad old days where Cromwell's Protectorate had closed all the theatres, suppressed sports and pastimes, forbidden drinking and partying, certainly thrilled Charles and his now victorious court: the play was a huge success and one of the King's favourites. Loyal to the King and a staunch Royalist, Behn is seen to glorify and celebrate the Cavaliers and, as I explored further, I began to see glimpses of a more personal journey. One of the possible inspirations for Captain Willmore – her 'Rover' – was her friend, lover and fellow poet: the libertine John Wilmot, 2nd Earl of Rochester. Another could have been John Hoyle, with whom Behn had a far from stable relationship for many years.

Above:
Faye Castelow
Right:
Joseph Millson

However, I believe the most likely source for Willmore was John Wilmot's father, Henry Wilmot, the 1st Earl of Rochester, one of the Royalist heroes of the Civil War. Like his son, he was a glamorous figure, but also a striking military hero who almost single-handedly saved the future king at the Battle of Worcester in 1651. Perhaps Behn used all the men in her life as inspiration, while simultaneously taking her revenge on the society these men helped create the conditions for – a society that denied opportunity to women and eventually came to denigrate her own career.

Behn's carnival setting was a vital ingredient in her play's success. The early pagan Saturnalian festivals of Roman times, on which later Christian carnivals are based, were characterised by role reversal, feasting and partying. For a brief period of time, all normal codes of behaviour were overturned and continual partying, overeating, drunkenness and gambling were the norm. The status quo was inverted: slaves were treated to banquets usually reserved for their masters, and masters waited on their servants. Criticism of, and mischief towards, anyone in authority could happen without fear of punishment. In this

topsy-turvy world of disguise and free speech, Behn could give her women stronger voices, and more sexual freedom and expression than most were afforded. Unlike the women of most Restoration comedies, Hellena, Florinda and Valeria are not restricted to salons. The setting provides them with the opportunity to disguise themselves, escape into the carnival and 'ramble'; challenging the men who govern their lives, outdoing them and taking control of their own destinies – something denied many women in Restoration England.

In the world of *The Rover*, the girls strive to decide their own fate and fight for their dreams. Valeria concludes their journey with the question: 'For God or the Captain?' 'The Captain! The Captain!' is the resounding, winning cry. If only real life had been so straightforward for Behn and her female contemporaries. Perhaps Behn's brilliance is also in her irony – it is the young, inexperienced virgin Hellena who is the pragmatist and who ultimately gets her man, and the seasoned courtesan Angellica, the unexpected romantic, who doesn't. It may not be a coincidence that Angellica Bianca's initials are the same as Behn's. She captured brilliantly the heartbeat and essence of Restoration England, when the fashionable accessories for a man were his sword and his whore, while simultaneously nodding to a romantic, recent past. Yet Behn was, above everything, remarkably ahead of her time.

Loveday Ingram, Director

'Abounds with **industrial quantities** of **zest**'

Daily Telegraph

'The **sheer ambition** of the piece and its **plea for compassion** in a rapacious world is beyond reproach'

Sunday Times

THE SEVEN ACTS OF MERCY

BY ANDERS LUSTGARTEN

**24 NOVEMBER TO
10 FEBRUARY 2017
SWAN THEATRE**

Associate Director Alex Thorpe talks to playwright Anders Lustgarten and Director Erica Whyman about Naples, Liverpool and austerity.

How has the play changed during its development?

Erica Whyman: When I first read the play, this country was ignoring the scale of poverty and inequality, and merrily pursuing austerity policies. It spoke to me about that, and what we can do about it through art. How can we communicate the things that are broken in our society? Since then, the shift in the world through, most vividly, the EU referendum, has exposed some of that injustice – it's on our lips in a different way. What are the divisions in our society? Why were people so keen to leave the European Union?

*Tom Georgeson,
TJ Jones
Inset:
Patrick O'Kane*

The play wasn't always as explicitly about housing as it is now: it looked at a number of neglected groups in society. What all those groups had in common was a fragility in the housing provision, whether through high private rents, or city councils being leant on by central government to sell old stock in exchange for cash to build new houses. Building houses doesn't necessarily result in new social housing, so can make the most vulnerable people homeless.
Anders Lustgarten: Really, you can't overwrite or exaggerate the malice inherent in government social policy. An extraordinary example is that the one plot element that wasn't true when I wrote the play – Leon being subject to the bedroom tax even though he's an OAP – became law in between me writing the draft and rehearsal. I think that tells you something about social policy.

You've both talked about austerity. But why, in 2016, did it become such an important conversation to have?
EW: If you'd asked me that when I lived in Newcastle in 2011, I would have said that it wasn't under the covers

Above:
Patrick O'Kane
Right:
Allison McKenzie

there, or in cities like Liverpool, Birmingham, Glasgow and Belfast. It's the conversation that everyone has been having since at least 2010. You're right, though, that the south of England, Westminster and our broadcast media have become more interested.

I think it takes about six years to systematically change the structure at the bottom of the pyramid. The benefit system, in particular, has changed dramatically in these six years. The desperate fallout of those changes is becoming clear to us now. You can spin a good line for a while, that what you're doing is getting people into employment. But what if, by doing so, you make it impossible for someone to live with a roof over their head; to feed their children; to heat their house in winter; just because, for whatever reason, they can't work? AL: The wider context is Brexit, and people's social rage. People look at Brexit as being about race, but it's driven by many things. One of them is 40 years of the same neo-liberal capitalist system that basically takes away everything from people, apart from material wealth. Now everything is coming to a head and, inevitably, because the people who make political decisions are still in charge, the consequences are being blamed on everyone else. On migrants; on poor people who don't work; on Jeremy Corbyn – whatever. A lot of people are finding the courage to say enough is enough. People are looking all over the place for something else: whether that's in nationalism, or in unhelpful ideas about purity and nativism. I'm trying to look somewhere else – in human solidarity, in the potency of human connection.

The effects of austerity are seen in so many major cities. Why choose Liverpool? What is Liverpool's connection to Naples?
AL: Liverpool's got character. It's chippy and proud, emotional and energetic. With the docks, Liverpool could have literally shut the country down if it chose to – it had genuine power. That's the reason Thatcher specifically targeted Liverpool during the 80s: its prognosis was 'managed decline'. So, it's got confidence and courage and identity, but also a real sense of being cut adrift.

In Naples, there's a sense of belonging. It doesn't mean that everyone is having a great time, but it feels like a big, organic entity where everyone has a place. Liverpool has some of that. It's just like Naples – that same sense of connectivity, energy and violence.

In the early 17th century, Naples was the hub of an entire empire. There were a lot of people coming in and out. The Pio Monte della Misericordia church [which commissioned Caravaggio to paint *The Seven Acts of Mercy*] was set up to respond to the rapid social changes that commercialism brought to Naples, particularly the sheer number of poor people – the *lazzari*, the lepers – who were cast aside. That has relevance to contemporary Liverpool, which was managed into decline and is now regenerating itself in certain places. It's interesting, that juxtaposition of poverty and wealth.

Patrick O'Kane

The play could come across as two stories: Bootle and Naples. How do the two worlds link together?

EW: The thing that really links them is religion. Of all the English cities, Liverpool is probably the one where the sense of Protestant/Catholic loyalty and faith still rings loudly. In 17th-century Naples, Anders suggests a brutal and honest relationship between the Church and the state – it comes in for quite a beating. Yet, to me, these stories are united by those tenets of Christianity that go beyond the Church – genuine compassion, charity and love. In the Bootle story, the characters need to work out how to love each other. In Naples, Caravaggio is a man who is very hard to love. Anders paints a thrilling and beautiful picture of what that looks and feels like. Love connects the two storylines. It's about people, and if we get it right, it moves us beyond the political context.

What drew you to the work of Caravaggio?

AL: He's just a banger, isn't he? A few Caravaggio experts have said he's a very 'easy' artist. What he's doing is highly technical – with chiaroscuro, the angles, the structure – but he makes it looks easy. The best comparison is to an athlete. Look at the footballer Mesut Özil and how he controls a long ball. It looks easy, but you try it. What Caravaggio is doing is a political act – making something accessible to normal people. Most of the time, people try to keep their job, their power. But Caravaggio believed you didn't need to do that – it's apparent what's going on in his work immediately. That's exciting and, politically, admirable.
EW: Having the opportunity to look at Caravaggio's work in the context of his contemporaries, and to think about the relationship he had with the Church, the Bible and the subjects of his paintings, has completely transformed my understanding. His paintings are radical explosions of love.

Caravaggio is often described as being brutish and violent. How do you present such a potentially unlikeable character for the stage?

AL: My play is not the conventional biopic. Caravaggio is obviously a genius, but tortured, and not immediately pleasant. I want to resist the temptation to deify someone who we regard highly. Doing that also sets up the possibility that you'll see them when their defences come down. It's more emotional, more intense – as we see in his relationship with Lavinia.

Finally, why is it important that the RSC produced this play?

EW: The accusation is often made, sometimes rightly, that theatre makers are preaching to the converted. But I think people misunderstand the Stratford audience. I am enthralled by their diversity and radical politics. The political conscience in this place has been alive and kicking for a long time. Our audience is used to being taken to Verona, Cyprus, Milan or a magical island, every week. They understand that Naples stands for Liverpool, for Merseyside, for Birmingham, for our world. Shakespeare would have found Caravaggio fascinating, and we have a responsibility to tell the most urgent stories of our time.
Alex Thorpe, Associate Director

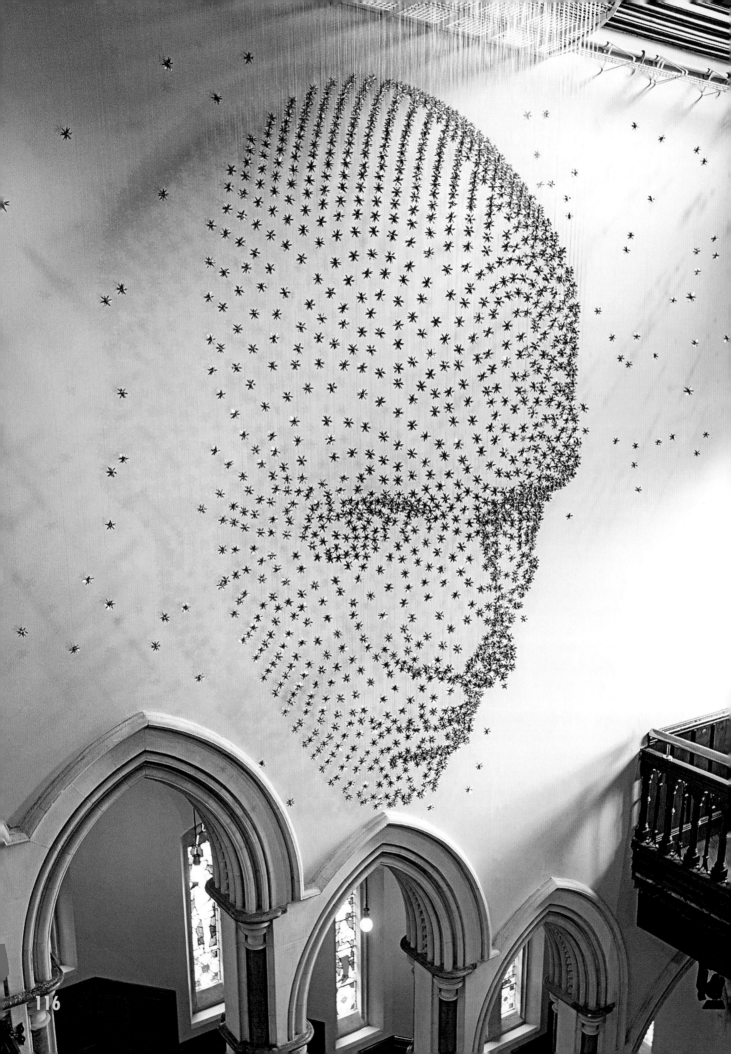

THE SWAN WING

In 2016 we restored the Swan Wing, the oldest part of our theatre estate, and opened a new exhibition for families.

Built in 1879, the Swan Wing is Grade II listed and the oldest part of the RSC's theatres in Stratford-upon-Avon. Originally part of the Shakespeare Memorial Theatre that comprised a theatre, library, reading room and picture gallery, it was designed so that visitors could immerse themselves in both the study and performance of Shakespeare. A fire in 1926 destroyed the theatre but, happily, the library, reading room and picture gallery survived, being joined by the Swan Theatre in 1986.

The Swan Wing is a beautiful piece of architecture, but it looked unloved next to the transformed Royal Shakespeare Theatre. Over nine months we worked carefully to restore the interior and exterior of the building, from the stained glass windows depicting the 'seven ages of man' from *As You Like It* to the stone grotesques inspired by characters from *A Midsummer Night's Dream*.

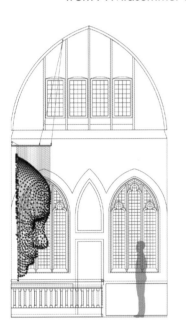

Work began on the exterior of the building. The whole structure was first covered in scaffolding and an enormous wrap to enable the roof lights to be repaired. Conservation work was delicate: some of the brickwork was cleaned with cotton wool; 200 bricks were individually repaired; and all the stained glass was painstakingly cleaned and enhanced. The theatre remained open throughout and, as such, careful planning and management was needed to make sure that noisy activity never interrupted a show.

The first stage of the interior project was focused on the public spaces and cafe. The cafe design included new lighting, oak panelling, a replacement bar counter and modern furniture: all of which gave the space a new lease of life. We created a cabinet of curiosities and built showcases in the walls for objects and anecdotes from actors to dressers to front of house assistants.

A major new artwork was commissioned, inspired by *Romeo and Juliet* Act III Scene II, where Juliet speaks of her star-cross'd lover Romeo: 'When he shall die, / Take him and cut him out in little stars, / And he will make the face of heaven so fine...' It is also inspired by the architecture of the whole building: the Victorian Gothic, 1930s Art Deco and 21st-century design. The title of the installation, by artist Steven Follen, is *For All Time*, a quote from Ben Jonson's eulogy to Shakespeare: 'He was not of an age, but for all time!'.

The construction of the installation was an engineering challenge: 2,000 stars were fabricated from sheet stainless steel, etched, hand-folded and then hung from a grid attached to the ceiling to create a three-dimensional representation of a human face. The installation is a stunning new addition to the building. The building, cafe and public space all opened to mark the 400th anniversary of Shakespeare's death on 23 April 2016.

Alongside this, we developed a permanent exhibition entitled *The Play's The Thing* for the reading room and old picture gallery, now the Ferguson Room, transforming these Victorian parts of the building into modern spaces that allow us to display museum

Left:
For All Time *by Steven Follen*

objects in the best possible conditions. We wanted an exhibition that looked and felt contemporary while housing beautiful historic content and giving the building a new sense of purpose. *The Play's The Thing* is aimed at families and new audiences and it was developed through consultation with these groups. We produced a range of interactive displays, using the latest digital technology mixed with sensory and tactile experiences – endeavouring to give visitors of all ages a hands-on experience and a way into Shakespeare. These include a digital on-stage moment with the chance to read lines from *Hamlet*; your chance to try on outfits from a virtual costume wardrobe; and touch-labels with fabrics, materials and textures to explore.

Above:
The Swan Bar

The restoration of the Swan Wing and,
bottom right, the completed exterior

The Chandos is the only portrait of Shakespeare thought to have been painted from life and was the first picture acquired by the National Portrait Gallery. This portrait was loaned to the RSC for the opening two months of *The Play's The Thing* and was displayed alongside our First Folio, which, in the 1700s, was used as a performance text and has pointing fingers drawn on to highlight key passages.

We extended the footprint of the exhibition to create a new space where audiences can sit and listen to oral histories from actors talking about their memories of performing in Stratford. Artist Vic Lee created a mural, inked like a bright red tattoo along one wall, to illustrate Stratford-upon-Avon and the RSC's riverside location. Little peepholes encourage visitors to look in and find archive pictures to highlight our local links and historic moments.

The exhibition opened in late October 2016, in time for the school half-term holiday, and was soon bursting with families and excited visitors. Feedback has been very positive, with visitors young and old enjoying learning more about our history, perfecting their Hamlet and virtually dressing up.

Geraldine Collinge, Director of Events and Exhibitions

The Play's The Thing. Creative design: Kossmann de.jong. Coordination and installation: The Hub. Building restoration: Shaylor Group. Architect: Mark Evans.

LOTTERY FUNDED

The Swan Wing and *The Play's The Thing* were generously supported by the HERITAGE LOTTERY FUND, TUBNEY CHARITABLE TRUST, GARFIELD WESTON FOUNDATION, DCMS/ WOLFSON MUSEUMS & GALLERIES IMPROVEMENT FUND, THE WOLFSON FOUNDATION and others.

The Play's The Thing is sponsored by UBS Wealth Management.

'Gregory Doran's
**magnificent
production**'
Sunday Express

122

THE TEMPEST

BY WILLIAM SHAKESPEARE

IN COLLABORATION WITH INTEL
IN ASSOCIATION WITH THE IMAGINARIUM STUDIOS
8 NOVEMBER TO 21 JANUARY 2017
ROYAL SHAKESPEARE THEATRE

Producer Sarah Ellis on how the RSC and Intel merged art and technology.
The technology and ideas presented in *The Tempest,* the RSC's final Shakespeare production
in this special year, respond to the ambition of Shakespeare's own time through the lens
of 21st-century advances. Theatre has always had a relationship with technology – whether
in the use of candlelight, the illusion of Pepper's ghost or projection mapping – and this
production championed that canon of innovation, while looking towards future possibilities.

Shakespeare, inspired by the cutting-edge advancements of his day and the masques
of King James I's court (spectacles of scale, ambition and creativity), included a masque
scene in *The Tempest*. So, 400 years later, Director Gregory Doran set us the challenge
of searching for what a 21st-century masque might look like, and finding ways to add
new dimensions to Shakespeare's most magical play.

> *'Shakespeare's masques were the multimedia events of their day, using
> innovative technology from the Continent to produce astonishing effects, with
> moving lights, and stage machinery that could make people fly and descend
> from the clouds. In one such masque, Oberon arrived in a chariot drawn by
> a live polar bear. So I wanted to see what would happen if the very latest
> technology could be applied to Shakespeare's play today.'*
> **Gregory Doran, Artistic Director of the RSC and Director of *The Tempest***

This challenge inspired us to think about today's possibilities. We found a YouTube video
of a whale projected onto a screen. The whale then broke through the screen, swam
across the room and created a spectacle for the audience. This clip, called *The Leviathan*,
was part of an Intel conference keynote. It's an example of augmented reality: the people
in the room saw the whale through their phones and tablets.

Inspired by this spectacle, we contacted Intel about our ambitions for *The Tempest*.
From this, we formed a two-year partnership and collaboration that has celebrated the
convergence of art and technology, and explored how, with Intel's expertise, the RSC
could break new frontiers in live storytelling. Put technology in the hands of artists, and
unexpected, unimaginable things happen.

> *'My team saw an awesome opportunity to help bring Gregory's vision alive.
> We jumped at the chance to explore the application of a new collection of
> technology tools. It's taken the best part of two years to develop this technology
> – and the measure of our success is when our tools disappear and the art is
> what we leave behind.'*
> **Tawny Schlieski, Director of Research at Intel**

Left: Mark Quartley

The notion of the masque was always our starting point, but during our first week with Intel, we saw the character of Ariel becoming a more prominent part of the discussion. We started to wonder if we could create a digital character on stage, in real time, performing in a theatrical environment and responding and interacting with the other actors on stage.

We then connected with The Imaginarium Studios, a company – founded by Andy Serkis and Jonathan Cavendish – that, with storytelling at the heart of its business, has pushed the boundaries of performance in film, gaming and television. Pioneers in the art of 'performance capture' (where an actor's work is electronically tracked and translated into computer-generated imagery), the company's creative expertise enabled us to think about Ariel as a digital character.

> *'Andy [Serkis of Imaginarium] comes from a theatrical background and he has always wanted to push the boundaries of what is possible with performance-capture technology. Realising an on-stage avatar as an integrated part of a theatrical production of this scale has been a mammoth development effort from our team. It wouldn't have been possible before now.'*
> **Ben Lumsden, Head of Studio, The Imaginarium Studios**

Creating a digital character for our stage has been an adventure and a challenge. All those involved have learned new things and discovered new possibilities. We have jointly used our expertise in live theatre skills, performance capture and technological capabilities, and combined them to create Ariel and bring him into the world of the play in a meaningful way. Led by RSC Director of Design, Stephen Brimson Lewis, Tawny Schlieski from Intel and a small team from The Imaginarium Studios (including Ben Lumsden, Silvia Bartoli, Bren Jordan and Dan Orchard), we have developed and designed a character who embodies Ariel.

Below and right:
The Harpy in development and as seen in the production

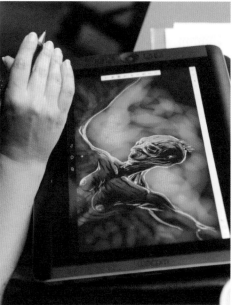

THE TEMPEST

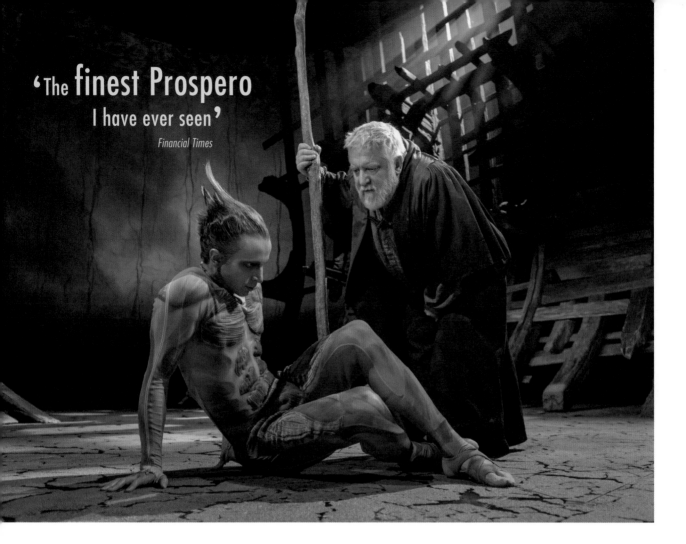

'The finest Prospero I have ever seen'

Financial Times

'Theatre is, by nature, a collaborative art. For the RSC, *The Tempest* has taken that to a new level, working with artists and technicians at the very top of their field. My role has chiefly been to orchestrate and channel all these talents towards a single goal and particular vision for the play. We were aware the technology was able to delight and entertain, but have been surprised at its subtle ability to illuminate and support Shakespeare's text, and to be truly alive and spontaneously reactive to the actor's performance.'

Stephen Brimson Lewis, Director of Design

The digital character you see on stage is not a recording but a live performance. Ariel is played by an actor, Mark Quartley. In his costume there are sensors picking up his movements: 'live performance capture'. Data describing his movements is processed, rendered into the computer-generated character in real time by Intel processors, and fed through to video servers for projection, live on stage. This is the point where the digital avatar comes to life. To make Ariel as real as possible, we have used facial and body scans of Mark. Using this data, Silvia designed characters (different forms of Ariel) based on Mark's physique and movement. The live performance capture from The Imaginarium Studios allows us to record Mark's facial expressions as well as movements, translating full performance into an animated character. With the combined skills of all three partners, we have powered the avatar to work seamlessly in real time, interacting with live actors and bringing a unique magic to the production.

One of the crucial aspects of Ariel working on stage is his relationship with Prospero. Earlier this year, Simon Russell Beale (Prospero) and Mark met for the first time in rehearsal. The actors' challenge was to discover and maintain a connection through movement, body language and eye contact. Those subtle physical elements were so crucial in making the digital character come alive in performance. Finding the connection between Ariel and Prospero in rehearsal was key. We all had to discover how the two characters acted together, in all of Ariel's different forms. Mark played with these ideas and established the rules of how Ariel worked on stage.

> 'Working on this production was extremely exciting, as well as challenging. It has been a steep learning curve for all of us. There were times it felt as though I had been talking in a foreign language all day. In the same way as the actors have had to learn how to interact with digital characters, we had to learn how best to integrate this technology, normally presented on a 2D screen, into the 3D space of the theatre. Fortunately, I worked with amazing technicians who embraced the challenge and we were able to bring the two mediums together.'
> **Pete Griffin, Production Manager**

As the year came to a close, we were able to celebrate the achievements of this two-year collaboration on the RSC's main stage. The show was made with the technology and tools of today in the hope of inspiring future generations. As Antonio says, 'What's past is prologue.'
Sarah Ellis, Head of Digital Development and Co-Producer on *The Tempest*

Designing *The Tempest* by Stephen Brimson Lewis.

The use of projected video in theatre is now familiar to audiences. Pioneered by the likes of Robert Lepage, it has become part of the designer's tool kit. Its insubstantial quality makes it wonderfully adaptable to our modern taste for swiftly moving productions and, of course, perfectly suited to the magical and dreamlike landscape of *The Tempest*. Working with Intel and The Imaginarium Studios gave us the opportunity to integrate this 'rough magic' into the very fabric of the play. My role throughout the two years of development became that of an orchestrator, or conductor, tasked with combining and editing all the various elements into a single vision. And the challenges permeated every detail of the design (including the costumes and wigs – Ariel had to support 17 hidden sensors, battery packs and transmitters).

Shakespeare's play throws down the gauntlet to a designer. A good design should serve the text and illuminate the story, and the guiding principle for me has always been that the process should be one of discovery rather than invention. If you allow the play to reveal itself properly, the design solutions should feel inevitable.

The rotting carcass of the Mary Rose suggested itself as a strong cradle for the action and perfectly suited the theatre's architecture. I knew from the start that I wanted to pull the set through the frame of the brick proscenium and envelop the audience with Prospero's island. Embedding the digital imagery within this semi-naturalistic set became central to my thinking, while the necessary projection-screen surfaces remained elusive and translucent rather than dominating the look of the production. This juxtaposition of tried-and-tested theatrical techniques – including a Victorian disappearing-table trick – with cutting-edge innovation is perhaps at the heart of what we hoped to achieve. The

Simon Russell Beale,
Elly Condron,
Daniel Easton,
Jennifer Witton,
Jenny Rainsford,
Samantha Hay

spectacular and magical could have its moment to delight and intrigue the audience but the human emotional impact of the play should never be smothered.

The ambitions for the non-digital elements of this production were no less than the digital ones. The semi-transparent underlit floor that appeared to float was an exceptional feat of engineering and construction, not to mention the enormous motorised 'mother grid' that supported the vortex screen structure over the thrust stage. Even without the projection elements, we pushed the boundaries of what could be achieved physically within that space. And the end result was a remarkable combination of all the extraordinary skills within the RSC.

Stephen Brimson Lewis, Director of Design

Pete Griffin, Production Manager, talks us through a *Tempest*-uous year.
For my part, 2016 was all about *The Tempest*. A new show, with cutting-edge technology, heavyweight financial backing and great expectation!

At the start of the year, we had already spent 12 months developing and exploring ideas of how best to incorporate the latest motion capture and digital technology into Greg's production. And so the year started with great enthusiasm, optimism and just a little trepidation about delivering all this, but we were buoyant. Then, on 10 January we learned of the sad death of David Bowie. On a positive note, we were reminded of the possibilities of original artistic invention and experimentation. Plus, we had an excuse to listen to *Life on Mars?* endlessly.

As summer approached, designs were agreed and signed off, and beautiful avatars arrived on shared drives with increasing frequency. Software developers started issuing bespoke plug-ins that worked. We left Skype meetings and conference calls with Intel and The Imaginarium Studios having understood 75 per cent of the conversation (an improvement!). Deals were made with hire companies. Construction drawings were underway.

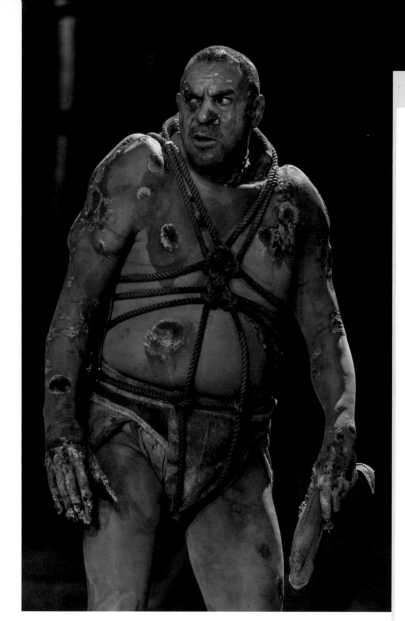

Above: Joe Dixon

23 June – the UK voted to leave Europe. Storm clouds were gathering. But *we* had 'cracked' Ariel's cloud (the object that would present the avatar on stage). We knew how to track it, project onto it, film it and fill it with smoke. We were on a roll.

As August came and went, some of us took a holiday, the rest just pretended to.

September brought the cold, harsh, dawning reality that two years on from the research and development meetings, rehearsals were starting and we now *had* to do this. But it was fine. I am lucky enough to work with amazing people, whose ability, dedication and sheer tenacity never cease to impress me. They were on board. They had bought in. They were delivering!

October was here and we were fitting up the show. As with any fit-up, it wasn't without its difficulties. But, considering we had to completely remove the stage and most of the balconies; hang 27 projectors and 28 motion-capture cameras; reconfigure the seating layout; build and rig a bespoke flying system on top of the existing one; and install a video and computer network more complicated than the one used for the *Harry Potter* films, it didn't go too badly. Quote of the fit-up: 'I was working on *Star Wars* last week but I've never seen so much technology in one studio as this.'

Into November, and the first audience. We dress. We tech. We preview. There's a Trump win. But it doesn't matter. We have made a ground-breaking show, but are too tired, too close to it, to realise.

As the dust settled on 2016 and all its unexpected turns of events, we had a chance to take stock and celebrate this production as a truly innovative show.

Pete Griffin, Production Manager

131

'This is a great **feast of mirth**
And you won't encounter a better
explanation as to why the RSC
matters than in the across-the-board
perfection of the performances'

Daily Telegraph

132

LOVE'S LABOUR'S LOST

LOVE'S LABOUR'S WON
(MUCH ADO ABOUT NOTHING)

BOTH BY WILLIAM SHAKESPEARE

CHICHESTER FESTIVAL THEATRE
OPERA HOUSE MANCHESTER
THEATRE ROYAL HAYMARKET

This year, the RSC revived its pairing of two sparkling comedies set in the shadow of war. Associate Director Guy Unsworth illuminates the process of matching *Love's Labour's Lost* and *Much Ado About Nothing*.

> *'I have thought for some time that* Much Ado About Nothing *was probably the lost play* Love's Labour's Won; *and to pair this with* Love's Labour's Lost *might be the way to find out. To mark the centenary of the Great War by placing each play on either side of that conflict seemed appropriate, but to find a director willing to accept such an exacting brief could have been a challenge. No one could have done it with more grace and invention than Chris Luscombe.'*
> **Gregory Doran, Artistic Director of the RSC**

In pairing *Love's Labour's Lost* with *Much Ado About Nothing*, there were countless moments in rehearsal when the two plays spoke to each other very intimately. The similarities between the plays are numerous: each centres on a witty, sparring couple, with peripheral characters that include a policeman, a curate and lots of domestic servants; both are set on a large country estate; music is integral – one finishes with a song, the other with a dance; they each feature masked encounters between their lovers, and any number of mistaken identities. In *Love's Labour's Lost*, the young men depart at the end to endure a period of hardship, separated from their lovers. A group of young men return from war at the opening of *Much Ado About Nothing* and proceed to win their lovers before the play is over.

So much for the superficial connections. To road-test the theory, we worked with the same company of actors, setting the plays either side of a war, and imagining them on the same country estate. We started by rehearsing the two plays in separate blocks to avoid confusion, but very soon felt that our knowledge of one play was informing our experience of the other.

Left:
Lisa Dillon,
Edward Bennett

CAST & CREATIVES

THE COMPANY
SAM ALEXANDER
JOHN ARTHUR
WILLIAM BELCHAMBERS
EDWARD BENNETT
PAIGE CARTER
REBECCA COLLINGWOOD
LISA DILLON
NICK HARRIS
NICK HAVERSON
JOHN HODGKINSON
TUNJI KASIM
EMMA MANTON
CHRIS McCALPHY
PETER McGOVERN
CHRIS NAYAK
JAMIE NEWALL
STEVEN PACEY
RODERICK SMITH
JAMIE TYLER
HARRY WALLER
ANNA WHEATLEY
LEAH WHITAKER

CREATIVES
DIRECTOR **CHRISTOPHER LUSCOMBE**
DESIGNER **SIMON HIGLETT**
LIGHTING DESIGNER **OLIVER FENWICK**
COMPOSER **NIGEL HESS**
SOUND DESIGNER **JEREMY DUNN**
MOVEMENT DIRECTOR **JENNY ARNOLD**
FIGHT DIRECTOR **KEVIN McCURDY**
COMPANY VOICE AND TEXT COACH
ALEX BINGLEY
DIALECT COACH **MARTIN McKELLAN**
ASSOCIATE DIRECTOR **GUY UNSWORTH**
MUSICAL DIRECTOR **BOB BROAD**
CASTING DIRECTORS **GABRIELLE DAWES,**
HELENA PALMER
PRODUCTION MANAGER **PAUL HENNESSY**
COSTUME SUPERVISOR **KAREN LARGE**
PROPS SUPERVISOR **MAGGIE NOTTAGE**
WIGS SUPERVISOR **MATT GEORGE**
COMPANY STAGE MANAGER
ROBIN LONGLEY
DEPUTY STAGE MANAGER
FRANCESCA FINNEY
ASSISTANT STAGE MANAGERS
HARRIET SAFFIN, GREG SHARMAN

MUSICIANS
PIANO **BOB BROAD**
DOUBLE BASS **PHIL DONNELLY**
DRUMS/PERCUSSION **MIKE PARKIN**
VIOLIN **KATHRYN JAMES**
CELLO **DOM PECHEUR**
FLUTE/CLARINET/ALTO SAXOPHONE
REBECCA GIBSON SWIFT
TRUMPET **ALEX MAYNARD**
FRENCH HORN **JOHN DAVY**

**REVIVAL CO-PRODUCED WITH
CHICHESTER FESTIVAL THEATRE, TRH
PRODUCTIONS, JONATHAN CHURCH
PRODUCTIONS AND DUNCAN C WELDON**

Despite the similarities in the two dramatis personae, they are clearly not the same people. For a start, they speak differently – mostly in verse in the first play, and in prose in the second. Our policemen couldn't be more unlike each other if they tried: Constable Dull's personality is suggested by his name, and he has 'spoken no word all this while', while Dogberry's verbal diarrhoea suggests he could learn a thing or two from his taciturn predecessor.

Similarly, one wouldn't expect the curate who is 'afeard to speak' in The Nine Worthies to be the assured voice of reason at the wedding of Claudio and Hero. Hence the decision to mix up the cross-casting, rather than suggest more links than actually exist. Pairing the 'matchless' King of Navarre with the villain Don John, for example, or the pedantic Holofernes with the urbane Leonato, provides the actors with distinct challenges and an opportunity to display their versatility.

Our lovers seem to require a different window of observation though. True, they have their differences: Benedick was 'not born under a rhyming planet', whereas Berowne is quick to 'woo in rhyme, like a blind harper's song'. And he's able to respond to Beatrice's injunction to 'kill Claudio' in a way that one feels the 'merry madcap Lord' Berowne could never have done. Rosaline wearies

Above: Sam Alexander, Leah Whitaker. **Right:** *Lisa Dillon, Leah Whitaker, Paige Carter, Rebecca Collingwood*

of Berowne's 'wounding flouts' but the lovers in *Much Ado* are 'too wise to woo peaceably', and their 'skirmishes of wit' become the very thing that makes them such a perfect match. But equally their emotional arc is so much more satisfying when the deferred union of one play is finally resolved in the other, and it therefore seemed wrong to deny actors Edward Bennett and Lisa Dillon the chance to carry the baton across the two.

Shakespeare completed these plays at least a few years apart, and so it's quite possible that they weren't intended to be a pair, at least not at first. The men's declarations of love in *Love's Labour's Lost* are dazzlingly poetic and exuberant, but are deemed by the ladies to be meretricious. And *Much Ado* reverses this by presenting a more mature and sardonic view of love, finally stripping back the wordplay and allowing Benedick to say, simply, 'Serve God, love me and mend.' But, in keeping with Shakespeare's antithetical thought process, it's conceivable that he deliberately shows us two sides of a coin with these two plays, and does indeed want us to view them as an extended double bill. The playwright readily acknowledges that the ending of *Love's Labour's Lost* is curiously unresolved – 'our wooing doth not end like an old play' – and the notion of the men waiting a year to win their respective partners is 'too long for a play'. So perhaps he felt there was something further to be said, and a few years later decided the labour of love was worth the effort after all.

Guy Unsworth, Associate Director

ROALD DAHL'S
MATILDA THE MUSICAL

BOOK BY DENNIS KELLY
MUSIC AND LYRICS BY TIM MINCHIN

LONDON
NEW YORK
USA & CANADA TOURS
AUSTRALIA

Executive Director Catherine Mallyon writes about *Matilda's* Big Year.
Among the 2016 anniversaries was the fifth 'birthday' of *Matilda The Musical* at the Cambridge Theatre in London's West End. The celebratory performance, on 2 November, with the production now the same age as Matilda herself, was attended by 200 children and young people from two London schools: Eastbury Community School in Barking and Beam Primary School in Dagenham (both schools performed as part of the Fairy Train in this year's nationwide tour of *A Midsummer Night's Dream*).

It was in 2003 that Roald Dahl's widow Liccy Dahl and the Roald Dahl Literary Estate approached the RSC to see if the Company would be interested in producing a musical based on the much-loved book *Matilda*. We were soon developing this wonderful story of innocence, wickedness, mischief, anarchy and love. The first production had a 12-week run in Stratford-upon-Avon during autumn 2010 in The Courtyard Theatre – now The Other Place. Those early performances were especially magical; audiences left the theatre, on occasion, into gentle snowflakes, spellbound, knowing they were among the first to have seen something special. The next year, thanks to philanthropic support, the London production was created and opened.

The same creative team, led by Director Matthew Warchus, have guided all the *Matilda The Musical* productions, wherever they have taken place, and have ensured that the presentation is always to the highest standard and remains as fresh at every performance as it was back in snowy Stratford. The production values and thoughtful approach that characterise all RSC work run deep through *Matilda The Musical*.

Since those first performances, it's been seen by 6.5 million people (and counting – around 4,000 more watch it every week) around the world. In 2016 *Matilda The Musical* spread its joy to Australia, Canada, across the United States and on Broadway, where it completed its near four-year, record-breaking run at the Shubert Theatre on 1 January 2017.

Audience members love to talk about the production, so we know that a recommendation from enthusiastic friends and family is one of the main reasons people book tickets. The production always gets high ratings for fun and enjoyment, energy and tension, engagement and concentration, and personal resonance and emotional connection. These responses help to explain why those who see *Matilda The Musical* consider it to have universal appeal, for adults and children alike.

Naturally, work with children and young people is an integral part of *Matilda The Musical*. Matilda School Resources is an online resource that provides information and

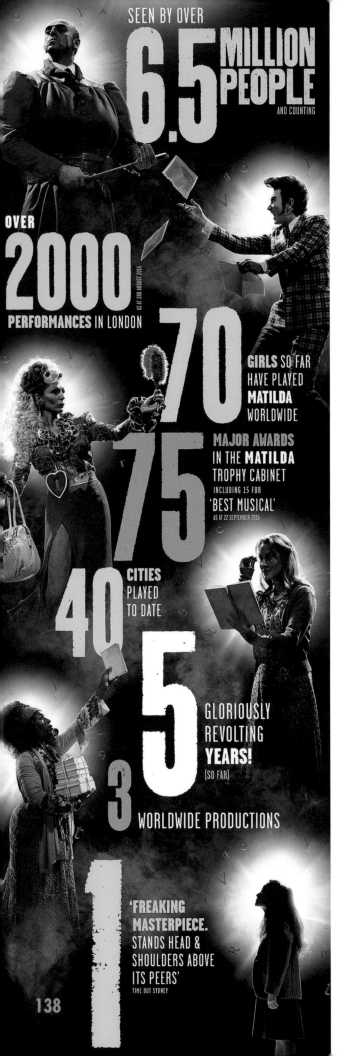

SEEN BY OVER

6.5 MILLION PEOPLE
AND COUNTING

OVER

2000
PERFORMANCES IN LONDON

AS AT 18 AUG 2016

70
GIRLS SO FAR HAVE PLAYED **MATILDA** WORLDWIDE

75
MAJOR AWARDS IN THE **MATILDA** TROPHY CABINET
INCLUDING 15 FOR 'BEST MUSICAL'
AS AT 22 SEPTEMBER 2016

40
CITIES PLAYED TO DATE

5
GLORIOUSLY REVOLTING **YEARS!**
(SO FAR)

3
WORLDWIDE PRODUCTIONS

1
'FREAKING MASTERPIECE. STANDS HEAD & SHOULDERS ABOVE ITS PEERS'
TIME OUT SYDNEY

138

educational content. In 2013 we set a National Writing Challenge, Write Here Write Now, inviting students aged between eight and 13 to write a scene or song set on Matilda's first day of school, and to introduce a new character. There was extensive nationwide participation and a specially devised performance of selected pieces at the Cambridge Theatre.

In autumn 2014 we worked with New York City Department of Education to repeat Write Here Write Now alongside the Broadway production. This programme reached teachers (who had their own RSC professional development programme) and pupils across the city, including schools in very challenging situations. One team, from a school based in a psychiatric unit, produced a particularly striking response to the writing project. They changed the story of Matilda's brother Michael (no spoiler – see the show, read the book) by turning him into an incredibly clever boy who conspired with Matilda to hide his genius, rather than alienating his family.

I write this in New York, reminded of *The New York Times* review from 2011: 'the best and most subversive musical ever to come out of Britain, nurtured into life by the Royal Shakespeare Company'. I'm sure the same sentiment applies in 2016.

Matilda The Musical is a big and complex show to stage. Many people work behind the scenes to make it happen. Everyone has their favourite moment and favourite song. As with Shakespeare's writing, there is something for all of us. As an audience member wrote, it is indeed 'a life-enhancing show'. Happy fifth birthday, London – let's see what happens over the next 400 years.

You can read about the RSC's extensive education work on page 88.

Photography of the London production of Matilda The Musical by Manuel Harlan

FINAL THOUGHTS

At the beginning of this *big year*, I was honoured to be invited to deliver the 40ᵗʰ Dimbleby Lecture for the BBC. Founded in memory of the broadcaster and journalist Richard Dimbleby, the annual lecture has been delivered by influential figures from the worlds of politics and business almost every year since 1972. The list made intimidating reading. It included a former President of the United States, the Director General of MI5, the Lord Chief Justice, the Archbishop of Canterbury and the Prince of Wales. I began to wish that I had clocked this impressive back catalogue before accepting the offer. However, this invitation to the Artistic Director of the Royal Shakespeare Company in Shakespeare's 400ᵗʰ anniversary year seemed to necessitate some sort of redefinition of Shakespeare's genius. So I began to look back at how Shakespeare had been celebrated and defined on his other centenaries, in previous centuries.

In 1864, for example, in the tercentenary of Shakespeare's birth, the French novelist and playwright Victor Hugo was exiled to Jersey because of his opposition to Napoleon III. Like a latter-day Prospero on his deserted island, Hugo wrote of Shakespeare, 'he is the sower of dazzling wonders... One feels, on approaching the work of this man, the powerful wind which would burst forth from the opening of a whole world – the radiance of genius on every side.'

In 1916, for the tercentenary of his death, Sir Israel Gollancz, Professor of English at King's College, London, produced *A Book of Homage to Shakespeare* in which Thomas Hardy called our house playwright a 'bright, baffling soul' and John Galsworthy described him as 'a tree of refuge', a definition that would gain in currency as this turbulent year progressed.

You may not be familiar with the speech from which the title of this book is derived.

> '... **the big year**, swoll'n with some other grief,
> Is thought with child by the stern tyrant war'

The chorus figure, Rumour, in *Henry IV Part II* spreads disinformation about a world that seems pregnant with conflict. He could be describing today. In the disunited world that 2016 became, it seemed we were badly in need of Shakespeare's words to articulate the overwhelming sense of strife and discord that, at times, threatened to engulf us. As Professor James Shapiro said at the start of our rehearsals for *King Lear*, 'I go to the newspapers to find out what is happening in the world, I go to Shakespeare to explain it.'

So, when describing Shakespeare's genius at the end of 2016, perhaps we do not need to reach for the rather pompous generalisations and grandiloquent hyperbole that these anniversaries tend to produce. Perhaps we don't need a new definition at all? He requires none – mainly because his mate Ben Jonson has said it all. In the dedicatory epistle he wrote for the publication of Shakespeare's First Folio, Jonson called his fellow playwright 'My gentle Shakespeare', 'Soul of the Age' and (one of my favourites) 'thou star of poets', but perhaps most memorably, Jonson said, 'He was not of an age but for all time'. As Shakespeare roars into his fifth century, that assertion seems pretty indisputable.

In the end, I decided all I could do for the Dimbleby Lecture was to respond with my heart and describe my own personal journey with Shakespeare. After the broadcast, I was overwhelmed by the number of people who contacted me to share their own personal stories of how Shakespeare's words have impacted upon their lives, and I'd like to share one of those stories with you.

It comes from a lady called Caroline, who wrote to me shortly after we opened *The Tempest* in the autumn. She was three years old when her parents moved to Hong Kong. Her father worked for the navy. He was 33, tall, charming and athletic, but he contracted polio in an outbreak that afflicted the island colony in 1954. Within a week he was dead. Her mother also contracted the disease and lost the baby she was carrying, a boy. Caroline remembers the navy burying her father at sea; his body, wrapped in a weighted sack and draped in the Union Jack, was slipped into the sea in Hong Kong's Deep Water Bay.

They returned to England, where her mother rarely spoke of her father again, except on one occasion. Caroline asked what had happened to her father when his body slipped under the waves. Her mother said, 'Oh darling, the sharks would have eaten him,' which was to haunt Caroline for many years to come.

Then, one day, at boarding school, they started to read Shakespeare around the class, and a girl stood up and started to read Ariel's song:

'Full fathom five thy father lies;
 Of his bones are coral made;
 Those are pearls that were his eyes'

From that time, all of Caroline's nightmares ceased, and she knew her father had merely suffered 'a sea change' into something 'rich and strange'. Years later, she, her husband and daughter returned to Hong Kong and floated little paper boats out into the bay to commemorate her father. On each was written 'Full fathom five thy father lies…' A touching farewell, and perhaps the most beautiful example of the power of Shakespeare to articulate our human story that I came across in his entire jubilee year.

**Gregory Doran
Yuletide 2016
Stratford-upon-Avon**

Gregory's Dimbleby Lecture is available on YouTube

Thank you to all RSC staff who helped to make this wonderful year possible.

CORPORATE GOVERNANCE

THANK YOU TO ALL OUR BOARD AND GOVERNORS FOR THEIR SIGNIFICANT SUPPORT AND GUIDANCE ACROSS 2016 AND BEYOND.

IN MEMORY OF
SIR CHRISTOPHER BLAND, RSC CHAIRMAN APRIL 2004 – OCTOBER 2011
IAN RUSHTON, RSC HONORARY GOVERNOR
DAVID BRIERLEY CBE, RSC GENERAL MANAGER 1968 – 1996
HOWARD DAVIES CBE, RSC ASSOCIATE DIRECTOR AND DIRECTOR OF THE WAREHOUSE 1974 – 1996
GUY WOOLFENDEN OBE, RSC HEAD OF MUSIC 1961 – 1998

* UNTIL 17 NOVEMBER 2016 RSC AGM MEETING † FROM 17 NOVEMBER 2016 RSC AGM MEETING

MANAGING EDITOR
REBECCA CRANE

DESIGNER
DANIEL BUDDEN, FYREFLYGRAPHICS

ASSOCIATE EDITOR
KEVIN WRIGHT

DESIGN CONSULTANT
ANDY WILLIAMS

PRINT CONSULTANT
GINA PRINT

THANKS TO: **SIMON ASH, CLAIRE BIRCH, MATT BOSS, JANE ELLIS, KATE GODFREY, SARAH PEAK, BECKIE RODGERS**

MIX
Paper from responsible sources
FSC www.fsc.org FSC® C020704

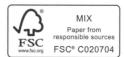

PRINTED AND BOUND IN GREAT BRITAIN BY GREENSHIRES GROUP, LEICESTER

NEW VANGUARD 275

RUSSIAN BATTLESHIPS AND CRUISERS OF THE RUSSO-JAPANESE WAR

MARK LARDAS   ILLUSTRATED BY PAUL WRIGHT

OSPREY PUBLISHING

Bloomsbury Publishing Plc

PO Box 883, Oxford, OX1 9PL, UK

1385 Broadway, 5th Floor, New York, NY 10018, USA

E-mail: info@ospreypublishing.com

www.ospreypublishing.com

OSPREY is a trademark of Osprey Publishing Ltd

First published in Great Britain in 2019

A catalog record for this book is available from the British Library.

ISBN: PB 9781472835086; eBook 9781472835079;

ePDF 9781472835062; XML 9781472835055

19 20 21 22 23 10 9 8 7 6 5 4 3 2 1

Index by Fionbar Lyons
Typeset by PDQ Digital Media Solutions, Bungay, UK
Printed in China by Toppan Leefung Printing Ltd.

Osprey Publishing supports the Woodland Trust, the UK's leading woodland conservation charity.

To find out more about our authors and books visit
www.ospreypublishing.com. Here you will find extracts, author interviews, details of forthcoming events and the option to sign up for our newsletter.

Author's Acknowledgment

I would like to thank Bruce Biskup for help in getting some of the references used.

Author's Note

The following abbreviations indicate the sources of the illustrations used in this volume:

LOC – Library of Congress, Washington, D.C.

USNHHC – United States Navy History and Heritage Command, Washington D. C.

AC – Author's Collection

The following shipyards built for the Imperial Russian Navy:

Admiralty	Admiralty Shipyard, Saint Petersburg, Russia
Baltic	Baltic Works, Saint Petersburg, Russia
Galeryi	Galeryi Island, Saint Petersburg, Russia
Nevsky	Nevsky Shipyard, Saint Petersburg, Russia
Cramp	William Cramp, Philadelphia, Pennsylvania, US
B&W	Burmeister & Wain, Copenhagen, Denmark
La Seyne	Société Nouvelle des Forges and Chantiers de la Méditerranée, La Seyne, France
Le Havre	Forges et Chantiers de la Méditerranée, France
Germaniawerft	Germaniawerft, Kiel, Germany
Schichau	Schichau Shipyard, Bremerhaven, Germany
Vulkan	Vulkan yard, Stettin, Germany

Even though Russia was still using the Julian calendar at the time of the Russo-Japanese War, all dates are given in Gregorian Calendar. For those interested, the Julian calendar was 12 days behind the Gregorian calendar until March 1, 1900, when it fell one more day farther back owing to the leap year observed in the old calendar. All units are British because the Imperial Russian Navy used the British Imperial system during this period.

Author's Dedication

To Janet Rose – my first grandchild, my new Janet.

CONTENTS

RUSSIAN BATTLESHIPS AND CRUISERS OF THE RUSSO-JAPANESE WAR

INTRODUCTION

Artist's rendition of the Russian ships sunk at the battle of Tsushima. From left to right these are: *Imperator Aleksander III, Sissoi Veliky, Oslyabya, Admiral Nakhimov, Knyaz Suvorov, Svetlana, Dmitrii Donskoi, Izumrud, Borodino, Vladimir Monomakh,* and *Navarin.* These were a collection of Russia's very newest and very oldest warships. (AC)

The Imperial Russian Navy ships that fought the Russo-Japanese War of 1904–05 were built between 1880 and 1905. They were drawn from the ships of Russia's Baltic Fleet. The history of the Russian major warships of the Russo-Japanese War was the history of its Baltic ships.

Russia required permission from the Ottoman Empire to enter the Bosporus with a warship, permission the Ottomans routinely refused. Ships from the Black Sea Fleet could not exit. To construct a Pacific squadron, Russia used ships built at its Baltic shipyards or abroad. Its two main Pacific naval bases, Vladivostok and Port Arthur, had only rudimentary maintenance facilities. Warships shuttled between the Pacific and Baltic in peacetime. Wartime reinforcement of Russia's Pacific Fleet had to come from its Baltic Fleet.

The ships assigned to Russia's Pacific Squadron when the Russo-Japanese War started in February 1904 were among the most modern Russia had: seven battleships and 11 cruisers. An additional eight battleships, three coastal defense ships and eight cruisers were in the Baltic or in transit to the Pacific when the war started. Unable to participate in the Black Sea were eight battleships and five small cruisers.

The naval war turned against Russia's Pacific Squadron. A relief expedition was tardily organized. The Pacific Squadron was renamed the First Pacific Squadron. A Second Pacific Squadron left the Baltic for the Far East in October 1904, by which time the First Pacific Squadron's major port, Port Arthur, was besieged. The Second Pacific Squadron contained Russia's very newest warships, some newly commissioned and still in the late stages of construction. It was filled out by ships in transit to Port Arthur when the war started, and older warships thought capable of fighting.

After Port Arthur fell, a Third Pacific Squadron was formed and sent to reinforce the

The triple-expansion reciprocating steam engine was quickly adopted by all navies, including Russia's in the late 1880s. Pictured is one of two triple-expansion engines aboard the coastal defense ship *Admiral Ushakov* prior to installation. (AC)

Second Pacific Squadron. Made up of ships rejected by the Second Pacific Squadron's commander, Zinovy Rozhestvensky, these were the oldest Russian Navy warships capable of steaming from the Baltic to the Pacific.

Warship design had been relatively static between 1650 and 1820. The introduction of steam propulsion in the 1820s, breechloading artillery and explosive shells in the 1840s and armor in the 1860s, and substitution of iron and steel for ship structure during that period resulted in dramatic changes in warships. By 1880 the warship had been redefined, but was still undergoing evolution. The Russo-Japanese War proved a crucial test of Russian warship design between 1880 and 1905.

DESIGN AND DEVELOPMENT

Russia did not upgrade to the 19th century's concept of a "modern" navy until 1880. Four technologies dominated warship design between 1880 and 1905: propulsion (steam engines and boilers), metallurgy (armor and ship structure), ordnance (including torpedoes), and communications (wireless telegraphy).

Russia proved an early adopter of some technologies. It was among the first nations to embrace the self-propelled torpedo, and had an experimental radio aboard *General-Admiral Apraksin* in 1899. However, operational implementation of virtually all new technology lagged behind the United States, Japan, and rest of Europe by five to ten years. This was partly due to Russia's inadequate industrial base, more primitive than the rest of Europe and the United States. It was also due to budget limitations and an Admiralty reluctant to implement new technology.

Warship development 1880–1905

The most important change in naval architecture between 1880 and 1905 was the triple-expansion steam engine. Compound steam engines, introduced in naval vessels in the 1870s, reused the engine's steam in a lower-pressure cylinder. Triple-expansion engines had a high-pressure, medium-pressure, and low-pressure cylinder. The high-pressure cylinder used steam from the boiler. The next two cylinders used steam exhausted from previous cylinders. (Some engines split medium-pressure exhaust steam between two low-pressure cylinders; although a four-cylinder engine, they still had three stages.)

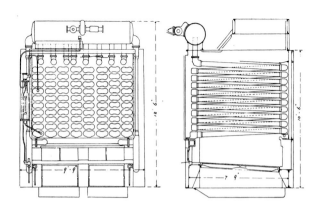

The Belleville water-tube boiler was developed in France in 1891, and quickly adopted by Imperial Russia to power its warships. This shows a rear (left) and side (right) view of a Belleville boiler. (AC)

Armor went through tremendous evolution between 1885 and 1900. A shot which could penetrate 10.4 inches of compound armor would be stopped by anything over five inches of Krupp steel or 6.5 inches of Harvey steel. The various forms of armor had the same density. Newer steels offered greater protection at less weight. (AC)

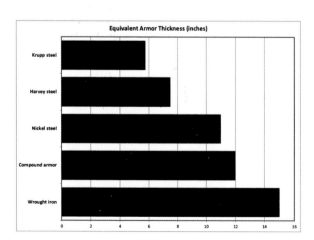

The Royal Navy first installed triple-expansion engines in warships in 1885. Triple-expansion engines roughly doubled the amount of energy extracted from the coal burned, eliminating the need for auxiliary sail propulsion. All navies, including Russia's, quickly switched to triple-expansion engines. All Russian cruisers and Russian battleships started after 1888 used triple-expansion engines. By 1904 it was mature technology. While some nations, notably Great Britain, were experimenting with steam turbine propulsion, Japanese and Russian ships then exclusively used reciprocating steam engines. All but Russia's oldest warships had triple-expansion engines.

Steam engines were fueled by boiler-produced steam. This period saw the shift from fire-tube boilers to water-tube boilers. Fire-tube boilers passed tubes filled with heated gas through a sealed water container. The marine version, known as a Scotch boiler, was a horizontal cylinder containing water through which flues passed.

Water-tube boilers passed water through tubes in the firebox. This provided more efficient heating, transferring more heat more quickly. France installed the first water boilers in a major warship in 1891. Britain followed in 1895. Japan started using water-tube boilers in 1897, with the United States following in 1899. Russia proved an early adopter of water-tube boilers in its cruisers, installing them in *Rossia*, launched in 1892, but did not introduce them in battleships until the Peresvet class, which entered service in 1901. Russia favored Belleville boilers, an established and reliable French design. Two major warships built in the United States, *Retvizan* and *Varyag*, had less reliable Niclausse boilers.

Armor also went through a dramatic transformation in the 1890s. When armor was introduced in the 1860s, wrought iron was the armor of choice. Steel was harder, but brittle. Hit hard enough, steel shattered. By 1880 compound armor – wrought iron with steel welded to the face – was the standard.

In 1889 nickel-steel armor became available. Adding nickel to steel combined steel's hardness with wrought iron's toughness. While only a little more resistant than compound armor, it was simpler, cheaper, and more reliable. In 1890 Harvey steel was invented. It treated a steel plate, typically nickel steel, by exposing one face to carbon and quenching it with oil and then water. The resulting plates had extremely hard outer edges. In 1894 Krupp improved the Harvey process with a more sophisticated method of hardening the plate. Five inches of Krupp armor produced the same protection as 6½ inches of Harvey steel, 9½ inches of nickel steel, and 10½ inches of compound armor.

Russia started out using compound armor. It first used both nickel steel and Harvey steel in 1892, building *Sissoi Veliky* with nickel steel and *Rossia* with Harvey steel. The Russian Navy adopted Krupp armor slowly because of Krupp's formidable royalties to license the process. Not until 1899 were Russian warships built protected by Krupp steel.

Regardless of the armor used, the protection offered was adequate. No Russian battleship, even the "lightly" armored Peresvet class, experienced a penetrating hit by a Japanese 12in. shell. No Russian battleships were sunk by gunfire at the battle of the Yellow Sea. The battleships sunk by gunfire at Tsushima sank owing to runaway fires started by Japanese shells.

Naval artillery stabilized in the 1880s. There were continual incremental improvements through the 1890s and through the Russo-Japanese War but no dramatic changes in artillery size or performance. The 12-inch breechloader became the battleship main gun for all navies, with calibers (the ratio of length to bore diameter) gradually increasing. The big change was a result of dramatic increases in combat range over the period. In 1890, 1,500 yards was considered the maximum effective range of a 12-inch gun, even though it could fire much farther. Ships needed to be close to ensure hits. The rates of fire of large guns with shells nine inches in diameter or greater was slow. Theoretically, a Russian 12-inch naval gun could load, fire and reload every 90 seconds. In reality, three to five minutes between shots was typical.

The Russian Navy armed its battleships and armored cruisers with torpedoes. The 15-inch diameter torpedo was standard for these ships. Shown are torpedoes being loaded on the battleship *Tsesarevich*. (AC)

Fire control improved dramatically over the next 15 years, as did the desire to keep battleships outside torpedo range. At the battle of the Yellow Sea the two sides engaged at 15,000 yards. Both sides were accurate within 12,000 yards. Russian shells were filled with cordite, while Japan used the more powerful shimose powder (which used picric acid). Shimose powder increased hits' ability to start fires. It had no more penetrating power.

The standard torpedo for the Russian Navy had a 15in. diameter, and was powered by compressed air. Most other nations, including Japan, had gone to the more powerful 18in. torpedo. To a large extent, this did not matter. No Russian battleship or cruiser managed to hit a Japanese warship with a torpedo.

The final technology affecting the Russo-Japanese War was radio or wireless. The first broadcast radio stations were established in 1897. By 1902 Marconi began testing radio aboard ships. By 1904 Japan had radios on scout cruisers. A radio-equipped cruiser warned Admiral Togo of the Russian fleet's entry into the Tsushima Strait, allowing Togo to intercept the Russians as they exited the strait.

Russia installed a radio broadcast station on *General-Admiral Apraksin* in 1899 after *Apraksin* ran aground in that November. The radio was used to coordinate salvage efforts. Despite this, the experiment was not expanded. Radios were not installed operationally until the Russo-Japanese War, and then only on a few cruisers.

Through most of the 1880s Russia's primary naval foe was Great Britain. Its battle fleet existed to protect the Russian coasts along the Baltic and

When *General-Admiral Apraksin* ran aground in November 1899 the Russian Navy installed an experimental wireless to help with salvage efforts. Despite the utility of this "wireless telegraph" during salvage efforts, Russia failed to pursue installing wireless aboard ships until the Russo-Japanese War started. (AC)

Black Seas, where the cruisers were to conduct commerce raiding against Britain's mercantile fleet. Its battleships were designed to operate short ranges in sheltered seas, while cruisers were built for long range over open ocean.

In the early 1890s Russia realized its cruisers might get trapped in frozen ports if war started in the winter. Russia sought an ice-free Pacific port in Korea or China. Securing Port Arthur on China's Liaodong Peninsula in 1897 meant Russia needed a battle fleet to defend it. Russian battleships built after the mid-1890s reflected this shift, being built with higher freeboard to operate in oceanic waters and with longer range to allow the ships to transit between the Baltic and the Pacific.

Battleships and coastal defense ships

The Imperial Russian Navy built only one battleship prior to 1880: *Petr Velikkii*, completed in 1876. *Velikkii* belonged to the first generation of seagoing ironclads such as Britain's *Warrior* or France's *Gloire*. Naval architecture advanced so quickly that it was obsolescent in 1869 when laid down and obsolete when it entered service. Russia built no more battleships until the middle of the 1880s, with the three-ship Ekaterina II class in the Black Sea and *Imperator Nikolai I* in the Black Sea.

Imperator Nikolai I carried a main battery of 12in. guns mounted centerline in a twin-gun turret in a fully enclosed turret. It carried a mixed secondary battery with four 9-inch and eight 6-inch guns on broadside mountings. To protect against torpedo boats it was armed with five Gatling-style 5-barreled 3-pounder (47mm) guns on each broadside. Finally, it carried five torpedo tubes: two fixed tubes on each broadside (one forward

 THE TORPEDO ROOM

Both Russian and Japanese battleships and armored cruisers of the Russo-Japanese war carried torpedo tubes. They were always fixed in the hull and always single mounts. The ship had to be aimed when firing a torpedo. This meant the broadside torpedoes were always launched perpendicular to the direction the ship was traveling. While the single torpedo tube mounted in the bow or stern (when carried) was always mounted above a ship's waterline, some broadside torpedoes were mounted in tubes that opened below the waterline. This avoided the shock of a torpedo hitting the water when launched from a deck-mounted tube, theoretically improving the accuracy and increasing the miniscule chance a single torpedo might actually hit a target.

This plate shows the torpedo room in which a broadside, below-water torpedo tube is mounted. A team of sailors is loading a torpedo into the single tube. At this point the outer door of the torpedo tube is closed. Once the torpedo is slid into the tube and the outer door sealed, the outer door is opened and the torpedo launched.

In 1904 the standard Russian torpedo was 15 inches in diameter, and powered by compressed air that ran through a turbine that moved the propeller. It had a warhead of around 200 pounds. This was enough to punch a hole in any ship, but while a single hit would be disabling, it was unlikely to sink a battleship or armored cruiser.

Torpedoes were also short-range weapons. In 1905 Russian torpedoes could travel only 1,000 yards. Admirals preferred that their expensive battleships fight at ranges where fire from smaller ships could not reach the battleships. Since battleships exchanged fire at ranges typically between 5,000 and 12,000 yards during the Russo-Japanese War, opportunities for battleships to fire torpedoes were rare.

and one aft on each side) and a fixed tube firing aft. It had a compound steam engine and was protected by compound armor, both standard when construction started.

Imperator Nikolai I was the template for all subsequent Imperial Russian battleship and coastal defense ships until the dreadnought era. Except for the Peresvet class and Russian coastal defense ships (armed with 10-inch main batteries), subsequent Russian battleships carried 12-inch guns. All battleships begun after 1890 had two main turrets to the *Imperator Nikolai I*'s one. Only *Gangut* (started in 1888 and wrecked in 1897) had one turret. Except for *General-Admiral Apraksin*, ships mounted two main guns per turret. (*Apraksin* mounted one gun on its after turret.) All main guns were mounted centerline. The Russian Navy avoided mounting main guns in wing turrets.

The mixed secondary battery was also repeated. *Nikolai I* carried 9-inch and 6-inch guns, and subsequent designs typically carried 6-inch and 3-inch guns. They were intended to compensate for the main guns' slow rate of fire. Secondary guns were intended to produce "smothering fire" suppressing enemy battleships' gunfire. A battleship successfully silencing its enemy could close and finish off its opponent at ranges where the slow-firing main guns would hit. Quick-firing 3-pounder and 1-pounder (37mm) guns were retained for defense against torpedo boats. The single barrel Hotchkiss quick-firing gun, introduced in 1886, replaced the more complex multi-barrel mountings in subsequent designs.

All subsequent Russian battleships and coast defense ships carried torpedoes. Torpedo mounts were fixed broadside or ahead and astern. Most, including all torpedo tubes firing ahead and astern, were mounted above the waterline. Occasionally a pair of broadside tubes was mounted below the waterline, one per side. The Imperial Russian Navy standardized on 15-inch torpedoes, although the Peresvet class carried 18-inch torpedoes in its submerged tubes.

Imperator Nikolai I and *Navarin* used compound armor. The coastal defense ships also used compound armor, probably because facilities capable of producing more modern armor were at capacity, with compound armor more readily available. Nickel steel was used subsequently (*Sissoi Veliky*, Poltava class), followed by Harvey steel (*Peresvet*, *Oslyabya*), with *Pobeda* and all succeeding battleships using Krupp steel.

Battleships built after *Imperator Nikolai I* used triple-expansion steam engines, rather than *Imperator Nikolai I*'s double-expansion compound engines. The Royal Navy introduced triple-expansion engines in 1885. *Nikolai I*'s engines had already been ordered by then. *Nikolai I* used fire-tube boilers, a practice continued in the coastal defense ships and

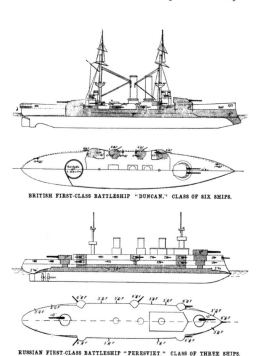

BRITISH FIRST-CLASS BATTLESHIP "DUNCAN." CLASS OF SIX SHIPS.

RUSSIAN FIRST-CLASS BATTLESHIP "PERESVIET." CLASS OF THREE SHIPS.

battleships through the Poltava class. Starting with Peresvet class, water-tube boilers were used.

With few exceptions, each class of battleship was more capable than the previous class. Armor got better, engines became more powerful and more reliable. Guns grew more powerful. Speeds increased, especially after the introduction of water-tube boilers. While *Nikolai I* was capable of a top speed of only 14.5 knots, using triple-expansion engines added a knot to the top speed of the *Sissoi Veliky* and the Poltava class. Switching to water-tube boilers gave *Peresvet* and later battleships a top speed of 18 knots.

Initially, the battleships that fought the Russo-Japanese War were designed to protect Russia's Baltic Sea coast, control the Baltic Sea and project power into the Mediterranean. These ships, *Nikolai I, Navarin, Sissoi Veliky*, the Poltava class, and the coastal defense ships were intended to operate in the shallow, protected waters of the Baltic and Mediterranean.

They had limited endurance. It was expected they would always be close to a friendly base. They were built with low freeboard, since the Baltic could not produce the large rolling waves of the Roaring Forties or North Pacific. Since they were expected to face the small battleships of the Swedish, Danish or German navies, they were smaller than the warships of Atlantic or Pacific nations.

In 1894 priorities shifted. Russia's increased interest in the Far East required upgrading its Far East presence. Starting with the Peresvet class, ordered in 1895, a new type of battleship entered Russian service. These ships were 2,000 tons larger than the Poltavas, increasing displacement by over 25 percent. They had higher freeboard, with the secondary armament mounted higher allowing use in high seas.

The Peresvets were the first class with water-tube boilers, permitting a two-knot increase in maximum speed. These ships had a 10-inch main battery, to allow a greater percentage of weight to be allocated to engines and speed. Initially they were labelled cruiser battleships, intended to combine the function of both. However, propulsion improvement soon made 18 knots a standard battleship speed.

While *Retvizan* had a lower profile than the Peresvets, both *Tsesarevich* and the Borodino class, intended to operate from Port Arthur, reverted to high freeboard and secondary guns mounted high on the hull. Except for the Borodinos, all battleships started after 1895 had an endurance between 5,500 and 8,000 nautical miles. The Borodinos' endurance was only 2,600nmi, closer to the 2,000 to 3,000nmi endurance of the earlier battleships.

While the Peresvet class was a largely domestic design, Russia designed its next set of battleships using assistance from France, which became a Russian ally in the early 1890s. The Peresvets were not completely successful, and Russia wanted to start with a new design. The result was *Tsesarevich*, designed and built in France. This design was similar to the French *République* class, with four 12-inch and 12 6-inch guns, all in twin turrets.

Russia's only shipyards capable of building large ocean-going warships were clustered in and near St Petersburg: Baltic Works, Admiralty and Galeryi Island shipyards. This is *Oslyabya* in the launching ways. (USNHHC)

BORODINO-CLASS BATTLESHIP

The Borodino-class battleships were the last pre-dreadnought battleships launched by the Imperial Russian Navy before the Russo-Japanese War. They represented the state of the art of Russian pre-dreadnought naval architecture in 1904.

The design of the *Borodino* was a development of the *Tsesarevich*, designed in cooperation with France and intended as a prototype for future Russian battleships. However, detailed plans for *Tsesarevich* were incomplete and would not be finished when construction was scheduled to begin. Instead the Russian admiralty ordered new plans using the sketch design of *Tsesarevich* as a starting point.

Five ships were started, the most battleships ever built to a single design by Russia. Four were sent to the Pacific as part of the Second Pacific Squadron, with construction rushed to complete them. The fifth ship, *Slava*, was not commissioned until October 1905.

Statistics	
Displacement	13,516 tons (designed), 14,091–14,181 tons (actual)
Dimensions	375ft 4in. x 76ft 1in. x 27ft–29ft 2in.
Machinery	2 vertical triple-expansion engines (2 shafts), 20 Belleville boilers, 15,800–16,300ihp; coal-fired: 787 tons normal, 1,235 maximum
Max Speed	18kts
Armament: Guns	4 × 12in./40 (2x2), 12 × 6in./45 (6x2), 20 × 3in./50, 20 × 3-pounder, 6 x 1-pounder. Torpedo tubes: 4 x 15in. (two submerged)
Armor	Krupp steel. Belt: 9in., deck: 4in., barbettes: 4–8in., main turrets: 10in., secondary turrets: 6in., conning tower: 10in.
Crew	826–846
Shipyard	*Imperator Aleksander III, Knyaz Suvorov* – Baltic; *Borodino* – Admiralty, Russia, *Oryol* – Galeryi. **Laid down:** *Borodino, Aleksander*: May 23, 1900; *Suvorov*: September 8, 1901; *Oryol*: June 1, 1900. **Launched:** *Borodino*: September 8, 1901; *Aleksander*: August 3, 1901; *Suvorov*: September 25, 1901; *Oryol*: July 19, 1902. **Entered Service:** *Borodino*: August, 1904; *Aleksander*: August, 1904; *Suvorov*: July, 1904; *Oryol*: August, 1904

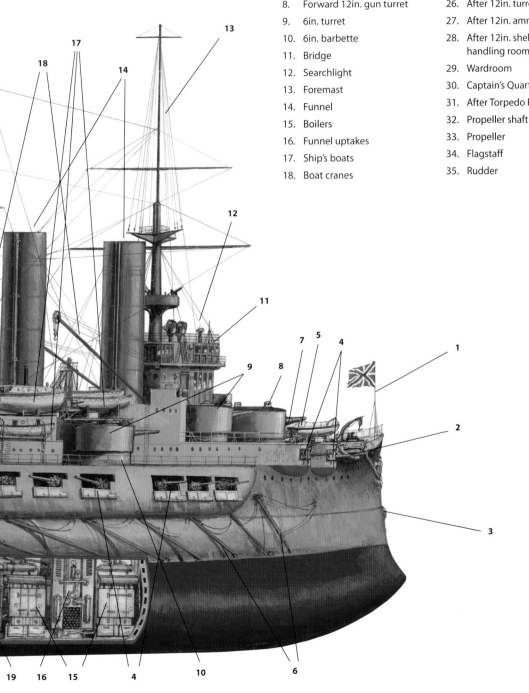

KEY

1. Jack staff
2. Anchors
3. Bow torpedo tube
4. 3in. gun
5. Ship's boat
6. Torpedo net booms
7. Forward 12in. gun
8. Forward 12in. gun turret
9. 6in. turret
10. 6in. barbette
11. Bridge
12. Searchlight
13. Foremast
14. Funnel
15. Boilers
16. Funnel uptakes
17. Ship's boats
18. Boat cranes

19. Engines and engine room
20. Main mast
21. 1-pounder (37mm)
22. 3-pounder (47mm)
23. After 12in. gun
24. After 12in. gun turret
25. After 12in. magazine
26. After 12in. turret barbette
27. After 12in. ammunition hoist
28. After 12in. shell handling room
29. Wardroom
30. Captain's Quarters
31. After Torpedo Room
32. Propeller shaft
33. Propeller
34. Flagstaff
35. Rudder

Tsesarevich was built in France for Russia to a design jointly developed by French naval architects and the Russian Admiralty. Its design was the basis for the Borodino-class battleships, Russia's final pre-dreadnought battleship design. (AC)

The main difference was that *Tsesarevich* retained the extreme tumblehome of the earlier French battleship design, *Suffren*. The tumblehome reduced the weight of the upper works, but at the cost of righting stability. The design was imitated in the Borodino class, built in Russia, albeit with less extreme tumblehome.

Although *Retvizan* was also built abroad, it was not a foreign design influencing future Russian ship building. While constructed in the United States, it was built to Russian specifications. Unlike *Tsesarevich*, *Retvizan* was not intended as a prototype. Rather, St Petersburg's shipyards were overcommitted. Russia needed more battleships, quickly, and Cramp and Sons were looking for business. It could be argued *Retvizan* influenced US battleship design. The Maine class, the first US Navy battleships started after *Retvizan*, were built by Cramp and resembled *Retvizan*.

Cruisers

Imperial Russian Navy cruisers, especially those designed and built between 1870 and 1895, were intended for long-range commerce raiding. Russia realized it could not build a navy outnumbering that of Great Britain or France, but believed its potential commerce raiding could deter France and especially Britain from starting a war with Russia. Two armored steel-hulled cruisers built in the 1880s saw service in the Russo-Japanese War: *Vladimir Monomakh* and *Dmitrii Donskoi*. Protected with substantial armor belts (4½ to 9 inches of compound armor), they could cruise under sail, and had substantial coal capacity (900 tons). Intended to operate independently on long voyages, they carried a large number of heavy quick-firing guns intended to overpower any enemy cruiser encountered before damage could be inflicted on the Russian cruiser.

A third cruiser built in the late 1880s, *Admiral Nakhimov*, shared some of their characteristics. One-third larger than the earlier cruisers, *Nakhimov* was initially intended as a second-class battleship. It was re-rated as an armored cruiser during construction, when 8-inch guns were substituted for the main battery's originally planned 9-inch guns. *Nakhimov* had triple-expansion engines and an impressive endurance owing to large coal bunkers, and also a sail rig that could be used for cruising.

Vladimir Monomakh was one of two armored cruisers built by Russia in the 1880s as commerce raiders. It had been awaiting modernization when the Russo-Japanese War started. This plan, from the 1886 edition of Brassey's *Naval Annual*, shows *Vladimir Monomakh* as it appeared shortly after entering service. (AC)

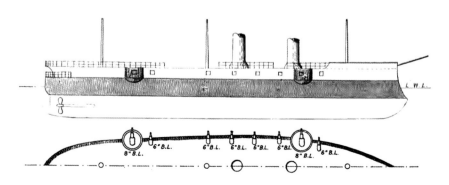

Russia's ultimate commerce-raiding cruiser was *Rurik*, designed in the late 1880s and laid down in 1890. Displacing over 12,000 tons, it was 25 percent larger than *Navarin*, a battleship started in 1890. *Rurik* was nearly 100 feet longer than *Navarin*, and one-third longer than previous Russian cruisers. It was heavily armed – a main battery of four 8-inch guns, 16 6-inch guns and 12 4.7-inch guns. Its armor belt was 10 inches of nickel-steel protection, reinforced by coal bunkers behind the armor belt.

Rurik was fast. On trials it reached 18.8 knots. It carried nearly 2,000 tons of coal and its steaming range was rumored to be 20,000nm. It was equipped with a full barque rig for greater range. These rumors led the Royal Navy to build *Powerful* and *Terrible*, cruisers even larger and more heavily armed than *Rurik*.

The threat posed by *Rurik* was less than imagined. *Rurik* would have been lucky to steam 10,000nm. The deck mounted guns were inadequately shielded. Following settlement of the Alabama Claims (prompted by the Confederate commerce raider *Alabama*), new neutrality laws made operating out of neutral ports and commerce raiding more difficult. Construction took so long *Rurik* was outdated when it finally entered service.

Rurik dominated Imperial Russian cruiser design in the 1890s. *Rossia* and *Gromboi* were updated Ruriks, eliminating the sailing rig, and substituting Belleville boilers for *Rurik*'s fire-tube boilers. They replaced *Rurik*'s nickel-steel armor with Harvey armor, permitting protection equivalent to *Rurik* over a much wider area for the same weight of metal. Intended as commerce raiders, both copied *Rurik*'s mix of four 8-inch, 16 6-inch, and numerous anti-torpedo boat guns (3-inch, 3-pounder, and 1-pounder).

All three had three engines: a centerline engine for cruising and larger port and starboard engines when speed was needed. Cruising on the center engine with the wing engines shut was supposed to yield better fuel economy. Since the outside propellers did not freewheel, however, their drag when steaming on the center engine erased any fuel savings.

Russia abandoned the commerce-raiding cruiser with its next armored cruisers – the Bayan class. Only *Bayan*, the class's lead ship, was completed prior to the Russo-Japanese War. *Bayan* was ordered during the navy build-up of 1896–1902. Since Russian shipyards were full, it was built in France.

Bayan was a "squadron" armored cruiser, intended to scout for a Russian battle fleet. At 7,725 tons *Bayan* was significantly smaller than earlier cruisers. It had better protection and bigger engines than its larger cousins. The engines gave it better speed – 21 knots – two knots faster than *Rossia* and *Gromboi*.

The ship had half the 8-inch and 6-inch guns and half the range of the commerce-raiding cruisers. This suited its intended purpose of scouting for a battle fleet. Its main guns were mounted in armored turrets. After the Russo-Japanese War, Russia built three copies of this design.

Heavy armor protection and massive batteries were intended to keep anything fast enough to catch a commerce raider from damaging it badly enough to cut a cruise short. Cruisers scouting for a battle squadron stayed at

Rurik was rumored to have an endurance of 20,000 nautical miles. In reality its range under steam power was less than 10,000 nautical miles. Early in its career it carried a full rig of sails – the barque rig shown in this picture. It was the last Russian cruiser built with a sailing rig. (AC)

Bayan was the last armored cruiser built for Russia prior to the Russo-Japanese War. As with *Tsesarevich*, *Bayan* was designed in cooperation with France and built there. Three near-sisters of *Bayan* were built in Russia after the Russo-Japanese War. (AC)

sea for shorter periods, and could fall back on its battleships when necessary. For scouting, protected cruisers were viewed as more cost-effective than armored cruisers.

Protected cruisers lacked the armor belt of armored cruisers. Instead they had an armored deck intended to protect the ship's machinery from exploding shells. If they took damage, the armored deck protected the machinery. The ship could escape, even with topside damage. Protected cruisers did not need to smother opponents with shells to prevent return fire, so they carried smaller batteries, sufficient to screen battleships from torpedo threats.

Protected cruisers were cheaper and faster to build than armored cruisers, and carried smaller crews. After Russia decided to create a Pacific fleet, it ordered 11 protected cruisers. Seven were large cruisers between 6,000 and 8,000 tons, with a main battery of eight to 12 6-inch guns. Their speeds ranged between 19 and 23 knots. They could operate independently or with a fleet. These ships were used to show the flag in foreign ports during peacetime.

Five were smaller – between 3,000 and 3,500 tons, with speeds between 24 to 25 knots. They carried main batteries of four to eight 4.7-inch guns. They were scouts, intended to range in front of the fleet and use their high speed to race back to the battle line and report when they made contact with an enemy.

Russian Baltic Sea shipyards were filled by new construction, including the three domestically designed Pallada-class protected cruisers, so Russia ordered five cruisers from foreign yards. Rather than depend on one or two foreign yards, the Imperial Russian Navy ordered a single cruiser built at five different shipyards: *Askold* at Germaniawerft in Kiel, Germany, *Varyag* at Cramp in Philadelphia, Pennsylvania, *Bogatyr* at Vulkan in Stettin, Germany, *Novik* at Schichau Shipyard in Bremerhaven, Germany, and *Boyarin* at Burmeister & Wain in Copenhagen, Denmark. Each ship was built to a different design to specifications provided by the Russian Admiralty. Individual shipyards were encouraged to provide their own interpretation of the specifications.

The best designs, as revealed through operational experience, were repeated in Russian shipyards. Less satisfactory designs were dropped. Four more Bogatyr-class ships were eventually started, although only *Oleg* was completed in time to participate in the Russo-Japanese War. *Novik* was replicated in two Izumrud-class cruisers, both of which accompanied the Second Pacific Squadron to Tsushima in 1904.

A final Russian cruiser type of the Russo-Japanese War was the yacht-cruiser, a protected cruiser built not primarily for combat, but as a floating residence for royal family members. Two participated in the war: *Svetlana* and *Almaz*. Both were the same size and armed similarly to the smaller scout cruisers. They had spacious

In 1899 the Imperial Russian Navy began ordering protected cruisers as a means of quickly increasing cruiser numbers. It ordered protected cruisers from five different foreign yards, intending to choose the best design for future production domestically. *Bogatyr* was chosen as the large protected cruiser design. Russia eventually built four more cruisers to *Bogatyr*'s design. (AC)

accommodations for royal parties, compromising damage resistance. Both could serve as scout cruisers during wartime. *Svetlana* was built for Grand Duke Alexei Alexandrovich, General-Admiral of the Imperial Russian Navy from 1883. *Almaz* was to serve the same function for Yevgeni Alekseyev, Viceroy of the Russian Far East.

OPERATIONAL HISTORY

The Imperial Russian Navy that fought the Russo-Japanese War reflected nearly a quarter-century of development of Russian naval philosophy and ship design. In 1880 Russia was still absorbing the lessons of the 1877–78 Russo-Turkish War. The war led Russia to reevaluate its naval strategy and the purpose of its navy.

1880–1903
In the late 1870s the Russian Navy, commanded by Grand Duke Konstantin Nikolayevich of Russia, planned a three-part construction strategy: development of a Black Sea battle fleet, improvement of the battle fleet in the Baltic, and creation of new steel-hulled commerce-raiding armored cruisers. Most relevant to the Russo-Japanese War was the construction of armored cruisers *Vladimir Monomakh*, *Dmitrii Donskoi*, and *Admiral Nakhimov*.

They entered service in 1884, 1886, and 1888 respectively. Except for brief returns to the Baltic for repairs and refits, they spent most of their careers abroad. Occasionally assigned to the Mediterranean or show-the-flag cruises to North America and Western Europe, most of their service was in the Pacific, operating out of Vladivostok, while frequently visiting ports in Japan and China. The three were absent from the Pacific when the Russo-Japanese War started, undergoing refits. *Monomakh* and *Nakhimov* were still at St Petersburg when the war started, while *Donskoi* was in the Red Sea, headed towards Port Arthur.

In 1882 Grand Duke Alexei Alexandrovich replaced Nikolayevich. Alexandrovich oversaw the Imperial Navy through the end of the Russo-Japanese War, as it grew from a minor regional naval power to the world's third-largest navy by 1903.

Russia then viewed Great Britain as its chief strategic opponent. Turkey in the Black Sea and Sweden and Germany were seen as local regional naval threats. (Japan, Korea, and China were felt to pose no threat to Russian naval power in the Pacific, with Russia's then-small Pacific squadron.) Russian naval doctrine envisioned developing fleets capable of defeating the regional powers in the Baltic and Black Seas if Britain or France did not intervene. Britain and France had intervened in Russian affairs (most notably in support of Turkey during the Crimean War of 1854–56), and Russia wanted a naval means to strike at them should they do so again.

Commerce-raiding cruisers, with battleships to protect Russia's naval ports, were adopted as

In 1880 Vladivostok was Russia's major naval port in the Pacific. Its importance was at its greatest in 1896, before Port Arthur became available, but it remained a significant part of Russia's Pacific presence even after 1897. (AC)

Sissoi Veliky spent much of the 1890s in the Far East, being withdrawn in late 1901 for a refit. It also spent time in the Mediterranean. This picture was made in Toulon, France, in 1897, when *Veliky* was in the Mediterranean during the Cretan Rebellion. (USNHHC)

the solution. This required increasing Russia's Pacific naval ports, as the Black and Baltic seas were too easily blockaded, and its Arctic Sea ports were frozen over much of the year. Vladivostok in Siberia, a naval port since the 1860s, significantly increased its importance in the late 1880s and 1890s.

Russia began building battleships for its Baltic and Black Sea fleets after Alexandrovich took charge. The first Baltic battleships, *Imperator Nikolai I* and *Gangut*, were laid down in 1880, soon followed by *Navarin* and *Sissoi Veliky*. Russia also laid down three Poltava-class battleships. The early 1890s also saw construction of *Rurik*, which served as the prototype for Russian commerce-raiding cruisers.

Gangut sank soon after entering service, but the other three ships saw extensive service overseas. *Imperator Nikolai I* was sent to the Pacific in 1894 in response to the Sino-Japanese War of 1894–95.

The Sino-Japanese War served as a catalyst for a massive expansion of the Imperial Russian Navy. Japan's victory, which gave Japan the Liaodong Peninsula, made Japan a naval threat. Russian interests in the Far East now went beyond having an open-water base to use against Britain and France. Russia needed to neutralize the threat upstart Japan posed to Russia's Far Eastern growth. Naval expansion started in 1895. Construction started on the armored cruiser *Rossia*, the first Pallada-class protected cruiser, and the three Peresvet-class "cruiser-battleships."

Vladivostok froze over in the winter. In 1895, in combination with France and Germany, Russia forced Japan to return the Liaodong Peninsula to China in exchange for greater war indemnities. In 1897 Russia sent a fleet to Lushun (a port at the peninsula's tip). It leased the Peninsula from China in 1898, renaming Lushun Port Arthur. Between 1896 and 1900 Russia sent its three oldest battleships to the Pacific, reinforcing its cruisers already present.

C   **THE LAST STAND OF THE *DMITRII DONSKOI***

Dmitrii Donskoi was an elderly armored cruiser launched in the 1880s. It was originally equipped with a full rig of sails. It was modernized several times, the last refit ending in early 1903. (By then the sails were gone.) It was steaming to Port Arthur when the war started, but returned to St Petersburg. Assigned to the Second Pacific Squadron when it left for Port Arthur, *Dmitrii Donskoi* was considered one of the squadron's most incompetently crewed vessels. Largely ignored during the daylight phase of the battle of Tsushima's first day, it came into its own during the nighttime part of the battle. It fought an epic contest with Japanese torpedo boats and cruisers, sinking two torpedo boats and damaging another torpedo boat and three Japanese cruisers.

Dmitrii Donskoi was first attacked by several waves of torpedo boats, but drove all of them off. Two torpedo boats, probably Number 74 and Number 75, were sunk by the armored cruiser. A third torpedo boat was seriously damaged. *Dmitrii Donskoi* next beat off an attack by four protected cruisers, damaging three of them. Finally, losing itself in the night, *Dmitrii Donskoi* crawled off to the north, heading to Vladivostok. Since the Japanese fleet's only losses were three torpedo boats, it appears the over-age, out-of-date *Donskoi* was the Russian fleet's most effective warship at Tsushima.

This plate shows the climax of *Donskoi*'s night. Under torpedo attack by Japan's 11th Torpedo Boat Division, *Donskoi* is dodging the enemy's fish while beating off the torpedo boats with all the guns it can bring to bear blazing. The results of its efforts can be dimly seen in the distance, as several of its shots score hits on the attacking torpedo boats.

Russia's decision to take Port Arthur put Russia and Imperial Japan on a collision course. The port had two major parts: the Outer Harbor (bottom) and the Inner Harbor (upper). The Inner Harbor was divided into the West Harbor and the East Harbor, where the dockyards were. (AC)

With Russia expanding Port Arthur, construction went into overdrive. Russia sought a fleet with eight battleships and eight cruisers in each major fleet (Baltic, Black, and Pacific) by 1905. Baltic Sea shipyards had at least five major warships on building ways between 1895 and 1902, with eight slips occupied in 1900 and seven in 1901. To permit faster build-up, Russia ordered warships built in foreign countries. Not until the eve of the Russo-Japanese War was Russia near to achieving that goal, which was delayed because of the long period (typically three years) between a ship's launch and its fitting-out.

As new battleships and cruisers entered service they were sent East, typically transiting the Suez Canal, convoying other, smaller warships being sent to the Pacific. By 1901 Russia had enough new construction operating out of Vladivostok and Port Arthur to rotate its oldest ships back to the Baltic for refit and modernization. (Port Arthur and Vladivostok lacked significant repair facilities for major refits or modernization.) Russian warships also often cruised in the Mediterranean enforcing Russian interests, often opposing Turkey. During the 1897 Cretan Rebellion three warships were assigned to the Mediterranean, supporting Greek separatists against the Turks.

By 1904 Russia's warships were spending more time at sea than they had a quarter-century earlier, its serving warships all postdated the end of the 1877–78 Russo-Turkish War, and Russia had credible naval forces in its Black Sea, Baltic Sea, and Pacific squadrons. Its ships had shown the flag, served Russian interests during foreign wars, including the Cretan Rebellion, Sino-Japanese War, and Boxer Rebellion, and supported Russia's Eastern expansion. Yet Russia had not fought a naval war over that last quarter-century. That was about to change.

The Russo-Japanese War

The Russo-Japanese War was the product of Russia's eastward expansion colliding with Japan's emergence as a world power. Japan was willing to accept Russia absorbing Manchuria, but became alarmed when Russia appeared to want Korea within its sphere of influence. Korea made a natural platform from which to invade Japan's Home Islands. Japan could accept a neutral Korea, but not a Korea dominated by a hostile power, including Russia.

Japan trapped the protected cruiser *Varyag* at Chemulpo when the war began. This picture shows *Varyag* (right) with gunboat *Korietz* trailing behind steaming out to face six Japanese cruisers. *Varyag* and *Korietz* were forced back into Chemulpo and scuttled. (AC)

In August 1903 Japan opened negotiations with Russia to set spheres of influence, offering to recognize Russia's control over Manchuria in exchange for Russia recognizing Korea as within Japan's sphere of influence. Russia still viewed the Japanese as a primitive people, not comprehending Japan's transformation into a modern industrial power. Russia ignored the Japanese. In January 1904, Japan broke off diplomatic relations, attacking Russia in February.

Russia then had seven battleships and 11 cruisers in the Far East. Four armored cruisers formed the Vladivostok Independent Cruiser Squadron. One cruiser, *Varyag*, was at Chemulpo (today's Inchon), representing Russian interests in Korea. The remaining battleships and cruisers were at Port Arthur. Additionally, battleship *Oslyabya* and cruisers *Dmitrii Donskoi* and *Aurora* were traveling to Port Arthur as reinforcements.

Russia's Far East ships represented the Russian Empire's most modern operational warships. Five Borodino-class battleships were in St Petersburg completing pre-commissioning fitting out. So were Russia's three oldest ocean-going battleships and two of its oldest armored cruisers. The Japanese fleet had seven battleships (one an obsolete prize) and 16 modern cruisers.

The Vladivstok Independent Cruiser Squadron proved a nuisance by conducting commerce-raiding sweeps in the Sea of Japan and the Pacific. This shows *Gromboi* sinking the Japanese troop transport *Sado Maru* on one sweep. (AC)

After midnight on February 9, 1904, Japan launched a torpedo attack against Port Arthur, attacking before a formal declaration of war. The Russian fleet was lying at anchor in the Outer Harbor, unprepared for a peacetime attack. Most captains were aboard the flagship *Petropavlovsk* attending a birthday party for the wife of the fleet's commander, Admiral Stark.

Sixteen torpedoes were launched. Only three hit targets. Battleships *Tsesarevich* and *Retvizan* and protected cruiser *Pallada* each stopped one, but although all required repair, none sank. After sunrise, Japanese Admiral Togo brought the Japanese battleships and cruiser in to finish off the "crippled" Russian fleet. Port Arthur's shore batteries and all Russian warships returned fire. Togo reversed course and headed seaward, pursued by the still-mobile elements of the Russian squadron. Two more Russian battleships and two Russian cruisers were damaged in the exchange.

At Chemulpo, *Varyag*, with the gunboat *Korietz*, was trapped by Rear Admiral Uryu's 4th Cruiser Squadron as the war started. The Russian warships attempted to break out, but six Japanese cruisers forced them back into port. All of *Varyag*'s guns were disabled during the fight. The Russians scuttled the ships, blowing up *Korietz* and opening *Varyag*'s sea cocks.

To protect his fleet from further torpedo attack, Stark withdrew all ships to Port Arthur's Inner Harbor. He also sought to strengthen Russian defenses by laying minefields outside Port Arthur and the commercial port of Dalny, farther up the peninsula. On February 11, minelayer *Yenisei* struck one of its own mines, and sank. Cruiser *Boyarin*, sent to investigate, struck another *Yenisei*-laid mine and grounded. Refloated later that day, it drifted into a second friendly mine and sank, permanently.

The heavy units at Port Arthur remained inert through February and into early March. Admiral Stark confined efforts to improving Port Arthur's seaward defenses: laying minefields, increasing shore batteries, and conducting destroyer sweeps. Repairs started on the torpedoed warships. Japan unsuccessfully tried to trap the fleet in Port Arthur by sinking blockships in the channel on February 13, but *Retvizan* and shore batteries sank all five blockships before they reached the channel.

The battle of the Yellow Sea, fought August 10, 1904, saw the Japanese and Russian fleets batter each other with gunfire for over three hours. Despite numerous hits, neither side was able to sink even one enemy ship. (LOC)

In the Sea of Japan, the Vladivostok Cruiser Squadron, the cruisers *Rossia*, *Rurik*, *Gromboi*, and *Bogatyr*, swung into action. Breaking through the ice around Vladivostok after hostilities commenced, they launched the first of six commerce-raiding raids on February 10, sinking one Japanese transport. A second sortie, starting February 24, spent a week sweeping the Korean coast. Japanese attempts to intercept the squadron proved futile, and a Japanese bombardment of Vladivostok on March 6 was fruitless.

The Tsar relieved Stark, replacing him with the aggressive Stepan Makarov, Russia's most competent admiral. Makarov arrived March 6. Three days later the Port Arthur fleet launched a destroyer sortie, backed up by heavy warships, the first of a series of aggressive patrols conducted by the Russians over the next six weeks. When Togo's battleships attempted to bombard Port Arthur later in March, Makarov sent his fleet after the Japanese, chasing them off. These skirmishes, while indecisive, improved Russian morale and performance and wore down the Japanese.

However, the Russian became too predictable. In the second week of April, the Japanese mined the routes taken by the Russians. On April 13, returning to Port Arthur after pursuing the Japanese battleships, the Russian squadron ran into the minefield. Makarov's flagship, *Petropavlovsk*, struck one mine, which detonated *Petropavlovsk*'s forward magazine. The battleship exploded and sank, killing Makarov and 678 others. *Poblema* struck a second mine, but reached Port Arthur unassisted.

Fleet command devolved to Vice-Admiral Wilglem Vitgeft. The Port Arthur squadron returned to its previous passivity, allowing Japan to take Dalny and land Japanese troops on the northern end of the Liaodong Peninsula, in May besieging Port Arthur.

The Vladivostok Squadron lost *Bogatyr* in March. It ripped its bottom on an uncharted rock in Amur Bay. Damaged beyond the capability of the Vladivostok shipyard to repair, it sat out the war in harbor. The remaining ships launched two new raids in April and June. The squadron ambushed a Japanese troop convoy in May, sinking two ships and several 11-inch siege howitzers bound for Port Arthur, and captured and sank several ships in a June sortie.

In July it conducted a raid into the Pacific through the Tsugaru Strait (between Honshu and Hokkaido). Sweeping down the Pacific Coast of Japan, the Russian cruisers captured three Japanese transports and returned to Vladivostok safely.

Despite prodding, Vitgeft kept his ships in Port Arthur's Inner Harbor during the spring and summer. Every previously-damaged Russian warship was repaired by mid-June. The Russians outnumbered the Japanese by six battleships to four. (Two Japanese battleships

The cruiser *Novik*, after reaching Tsingtao following the battle of the Yellow Sea, attempted to reach Vladivostok. It was caught and hunted down by Japanese cruisers, trapped while re-coaling. (AC)

had been sunk by mines in May, although the Japanese concealed the losses.) Vitgeft attempted a sortie on June 23. Togo closed to challenge the Russians, but Vitgeft mistook Japanese armored cruisers *Kasuga* and *Nisshin* for battleships. Believing himself outgunned, Vitgeft returned to port.

By August, Port Arthur was completely invested, with Japan controlling most of the Liaodong Peninsula. The Tsar ordered Vitgeft to take the fleet to Vladivostok, and directed the

The first "battle" fought by the Second Pacific Squadron was a nighttime attack on the Hull fishing fleet at Dogger Bank. Panic allowed the Russians to convince themselves the well-lit British trawlers were actually Japanese torpedo boats. (AC)

Vladivostok squadron to assist Vitgeft's fleet. Vitgeft reluctantly obeyed. On August 10, the Russian fleet steamed out of Port Arthur.

The resulting battle of the Yellow Sea was a day-long affair with two protracted engagements. The first started at noon. The two battle fleets exchanged fire for three hours, while Togo maneuvered to cut off the Russian fleet from return to Port Arthur. By mid-afternoon Togo realized the Russians were not returning to Port Arthur. As the Russians steamed east, Togo maneuvered the faster Japanese fleet to block the Russians' escape.

The battle resumed at 0530hrs, late in the afternoon. Neither side's battleships took damage seriously enough to threaten a ship's seaworthiness. Gradually, both sides were becoming ineffective through topside damage and premature detonation when firing disabled guns. At 0615hrs, with darkness 30 minutes away, it appeared as if the Russians would escape.

Then two 12-inch shells struck the Russian flagship *Tsesarevich*. One killed Vitgeft and *Tsesarevich*'s helmsman, and a second struck *Tsesarevich*'s rudder, jamming it hard to port. The Russian battle line disintegrated in confusion as it followed the uncontrolled *Tsesarevich* through its turn. The Japanese, sensing victory, closed to finish off *Tsesarevich*. *Retvizan*'s captain took his ship into a solo charge against the Japanese battle line, which fell back. Darkness fell, with neither side having sunk a ship.

Most of the Russian fleet returned to Port Arthur. *Tsesarevich* and three destroyers headed for Germany's Chinese port, Tsingtao. *Askold* and a destroyer fled to Shanghai. *Diana* ran until it reached Saigon. All seven were interned until the war ended. *Novik* also reached Tsingtao, but, rather than accept internment, it steamed out at dawn, headed for Vladivostok.

Novik attempted to reach Vladivostok through the La Perouse Strait. High fuel consumption forced it to stop at Korsakov, a Russian port on the southern end of Sakhalin Island to coal. *Novik* was spotted entering the strait. Two Japanese protected cruisers were sent, arriving as *Novik* finished coaling. They forced *Novik* back into the harbor, where it was scuttled.

Having learned the Port Arthur fleet had sailed, the Vladivostok Squadron steamed out of Vladivostok on August 12. Unaware that the fleet had returned to Port Arthur, Karl Jessen, commanding the squadron, hoped to rendezvous with them in the Sea of Japan. Instead, Jessen encountered Vice Admiral Kamimura Hikonojo's four armored cruisers. In the battle of Ulsan, fought August 14, the Japanese sank *Novik* and badly damaged *Rossia*

By December 1904 the Japanese had siege mortars in place which could reach the Russian ships huddled in Port Arthur's Inner Harbor. This photograph records an 11-inch shell hitting *Pallada*. The ship to the right is probably *Pobeda*, also sunk by Japanese howitzers. (LOC)

and *Gromboi*, putting the Vladivostok Squadron out of the war.

By June, Russia's Admiralty, realizing the war was going badly, made plans to reinforce the Pacific Squadron. Admiral Zinovy Rozhestvensky was assigned the task of assembling the Second Pacific Squadron at St Petersburg and taking it to Port Arthur.

Four of the five Borodino-class battleships were rushed into commission for the squadron. Added to these were *Oslyabya*, *Dmitrii Donskoi*, and *Aurora*. Rozhestvensky then included the least hopeless warships within the remaining Baltic Fleet: battleships *Sissoi Veliky* and *Navarin* and cruisers *Admiral Nakhimov*, *Oleg*, *Izumrud*, *Zhemchug*, *Svetlana*, and *Almaz*. Rozhestvensky rounded out the squadron with nine destroyers and a fleet train of seven auxiliaries.

Owing to Russian inefficiency, the squadron only departed Russia on October 15, well after it would have been useful. The voyage was the stuff of legend and nightmare.

Crossing the North Sea, the Second Pacific Squadron encountered Hull's fishing fleet at Dogger Bank, England. The panicked Russians, convinced the fishing boats were Japanese torpedo boats, opened fire on the fishermen. Russian fire hit other Russian warships, which returned fire. Before order was restored, one trawler was sunk, four were damaged and three fishermen dead. Five were wounded. The incident almost sparked war between Russia and Great Britain.

Meanwhile the Japanese tightened the noose on Port Arthur. By September Japanese siege lines were five miles from Port Arthur. As Rozhestvensky inched down Africa's Atlantic coast with his most seaworthy vessels, the Japanese drew closer to Port Arthur. By December 1, its Inner Harbor was within range of Japanese siege guns. Between December 1 and December 11 the Japanese sank every warship in Port Arthur's inner harbor.

D

NOVIK

Novik is best known for its attempt to reach Vladivostok after the battle of the Yellow Sea. Arriving at German-held Tsingtao the night of the battle, the crew loaded the bunkers with coal during the remainder of the night and *Novik* steamed out of Tsingtao at dawn, well before the time limit permitted for warships to remain in a neutral port and before the Japanese could react to the cruiser's presence in the harbor.

Unfortunately, its boilers and engines were poorly maintained once the war started. As a result, *Novik* consumed coal at massive rates. Running low, *Novik* was forced to make a refueling stop for coal at then-Russian-held Sakhalin Island to reach Vladivostok. Since the ship's arrival was unexpected, coaling took a long time. *Novik* had just finished loading the last of the coal and was raising steam to leave harbor when two much larger Japanese cruisers reached *Novik*'s refuge. *Novik* tried running, but was forced back to port, where its crew scuttled it to prevent its capture.

Japan captured the part of Sakhalin Island where *Novik* had been scuttled at the war's end. Impressed by the ship's performance, Japan salvaged *Novik*, commissioning it as *Suzuya*. The replacement machinery dropped its top speed significantly, however, and wireless made its function as a dispatch vessel obsolete. Deciding the small, slow cruiser was valueless, Japan scrapped it in 1913.

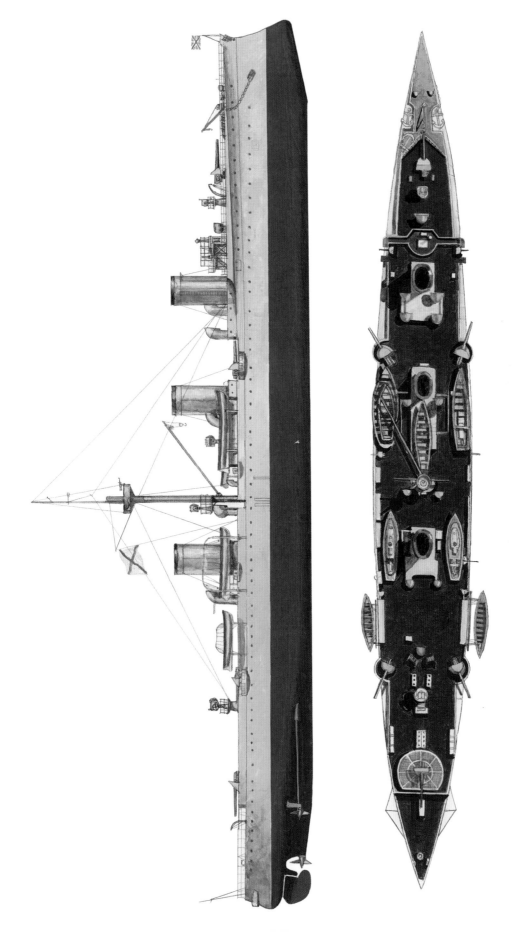

After Port Arthur fell, Rozhestvensky could have either turned back to the Baltic or pressed on to Vladivostok. He chose to go forward. The result was a battle in the Sea of Japan immediately after exiting the Tsushima Straits. (AC)

Only *Sevastopol* was still afloat. Its captain placed it in the Outer Harbor intending to steam to Vladivostok. Out of range of Japanese siege guns, but open to attack by the Japanese Navy, *Sevastopol* was attacked almost nightly by Japanese torpedo boats throughout December. An early attack damaged a propeller, preventing the battleship's escape, but the Japanese never sank *Sevastopol*. Instead, *Sevastopol* was scuttled in deep water on January 2, 1905, the day Port Arthur surrendered. Rozhestvensky had reached Madagascar two days earlier.

Rozhestvensky split his fleet at Tangiers, sending the older ships through the Suez Canal, and reunited the two parts at Nosy Be in Madagascar. He stayed until March 16, when he learned reinforcements were being sent, made up of the ships he had rejected when forming the Second Pacific Squadron. The Third Pacific Squadron included *Imperator Nikolai I*, three coastal

E   **THE END OF THE *SEVASTOPOL***

Sevastopol was the last of the three Poltava-class battleships built by Russia in the 1890s. Started in 1892 and launched in 1895, it entered service in 1900. Assigned to the Pacific Squadron in 1900, it was at Port Arthur when the Russo-Japanese War began and was trapped there after the battle of the Yellow Sea. The Japanese capture of Hill 201 on December 1, 1904 brought Port Arthur's Inner Harbor within range of the Japanese Army's German-made 11-inch howitzers. With their high angle trajectory, the 478-pound shells could penetrate the deck armor of any Russian warship. Starting December 5, the Japanese began systematically shelling the Russian fleet sheltered in the Inner Harbor. By December 9, all but one cruiser or battleship in Port Arthur had been sunk by the howitzers.

The exception was *Sevastopol*. Its captain, Nikolai Essen, took the battleship to the Eastern Harbor, out of range of the army guns. He intended to take the battleship out of Port Arthur and either rendezvous with Rozhestvensky's Second Pacific Squadron, then at Madagascar, or head to Vladivostok.

Although safe from the howitzers, the Eastern Harbor was vulnerable to attacks by the Japanese Navy, which was determined to destroy *Sevastopol*. The battleship thereafter was subject to incessant attack by Japanese warships. In late December, a torpedo hit and destroyed one of *Sevastopol*'s propellers, ending any chance of escape. The Japanese Navy continued its attacks through December, unable to sink the trapped battleship. Finally, on January 2, 1905, Russian land forces at Port Arthur surrendered. Hearing the news, Captain Essen took *Sevastopol* to the 30-fathom line and opened the seacocks on one side of the ship, to prevent its salvage by the Japanese. This plate captures *Sevastopol* as it begins its final journey – to the ocean's bottom 180 feet below.

During the daylight phase of Tsushima, *Oslyabya* and three of the four Borodino-class battleships (including *Borodino*, pictured here) were sunk by gunfire. (AC)

defense ships, the *Vladimir Monomakh* and an armed merchant cruiser. All were worthless. Rozhestvensky left Madagascar without them, not stopping until he reached Cam Ranh Bay in French Indochina. Inexplicably, he then waited there until joined by the Third Pacific Squadron.

Rozhestvensky's final leg of his trip ended just north of the Tsushima Strait, at the battle of Tsushima. Fought May 27–28, the battle was the most decisive naval victory of the 20th century. Japan captured or destroyed three-quarters of Russia's warships. The Japanese sank most of the newer Russian battleships the first day, hunting down most of the rest – as well as most of the cruisers and destroyers – that night and the next day. May 28 also saw the surrender of the surviving Russian battle line – *Oryol*, *Imperator Nikolai I*, and two coast defense ships. (*Admiral Ushakov* was scuttled.) One Russian cruiser and two destroyers reached Vladivostok safely. Three cruisers were interned in Manila and one destroyer at Shanghai.

Afterwards

Of the 37 major units of the Imperial Russian Navy participating in the Russo-Japanese War, ten were still in Russian hands at war's end. Four cruisers were at Vladivostok: *Rossia*, *Gromboi*, *Bogatyr*, and *Almaz*. Only *Almaz* was operational. One battleship, *Tsesarevich*, was interned, disarmed at Tsingtao. Similarly interned and disarmed were *Askold* at Shanghai, *Diana* at Saigon, and *Oleg*, *Zhemchug*, and *Aurora* at Manila. *Oryol*, *Imperator Nikolai I*, *Admiral Senyavin*, and *General-Admiral Apriaksin* had been captured by Japan at Tsushima. The rest had been sunk, many in shallow water.

After the war, the interned warships were released. Rearmed, they returned to Russian service. The three damaged cruisers in Vladivostok were repaired, requiring lengthy refits to repair battle damage and replace war-worn machinery. Only *Askold* and *Zhemchug* remained in the Pacific, the core of Russia's much-diminished Pacific Squadron. The rest returned to the Baltic.

Russia was faced with rebuilding its ocean-going navy. In one sense, for Russia the disaster was a good thing. The steam turbine and the dreadnought battleship produced another revolution in naval engineering, making all existing warships in 1904 obsolete. The fleet Russia had painstakingly built in the decade between 1895 and 1905 would have had to have been discarded and new ships built anyway. The lack of other ships and the slow pace of Russian ship construction kept these ten survivors in service through World War I, however.

A few of the ships experienced interesting careers. *Almaz*, the lucky cruiser that reached Vladivostok, was sent to the Black Sea. As it was viewed as primarily a yacht, the Turks permitted passage. During World War I it became a seaplane carrier. *Aurora*, transferred back to the Baltic, fired the shot starting the October Revolution leading to the Soviet Union's creation. *Zhemchug* was sunk by the

The protected cruiser *Aurora* survived the battle to be interned at Manila. Later, it fired the shot that started the Russian Revolution. Because of that, it continued as a training ship after most other Russian warships surviving the Russo-Japanese War were scrapped. This picture of *Aurora* was taken in Bergen, Norway in 1925. (USNHHC)

German cruiser *Emden* as World War I opened. *Oleg* was torpedoed and sunk during the Russian Revolution.

Most survivors served out World War I and the Russian Civil War to be scrapped in the 1920s. Owing to its role in the Revolution, *Aurora* was preserved as a training ship, surviving World War II in Leningrad (as St Petersburg was then named). Repaired between 1945 and 1947, it has since served as a museum ship.

The four ships captured by Japan at Tsushima were repaired, refitted, and incorporated into the Imperial Japanese Navy under new names. *Oryol* became *Iwami*, a second-class costal defense ship. *Imperator Nikolai I* was recommissioned as *Iki*. *General-Admiral Apraksin*, became *Okinoshima*, and *Admiral Senyavin* became *Mishima*.

Eight of the sunken ships went on to new careers, some in both the Japanese and Russian navies. To Japan, the Russian warships scuttled or sunk in shallow waters seemed an opportunity to increase its fleet cheaply. Starting with *Varyag* in Chemulpo, Japan refloated and refitted the Russian warships in territory controlled by Japan. This included all the cruisers and battleships sunk in Port Arthur's Inner Harbor and the cruiser *Novik*, scuttled in part of Sakhalin Island that became Japanese at the war's end. Four battleships and two cruisers were raised from the mud of Port Arthur.

All eight were refitted, rearmed, re-engined, and taken into the Japanese Navy as warships. To a large extent, restoring these ships was a false economy. Contact with salt water had destroyed the original engines and boilers. After long rebuilds at shipyard facilities that would have been better used for new construction, Japan gained eight obsolescent warships, better suited to the last decade of the 19th century than the decade after their commissioning as Japanese warships. Their only real value was their prestige as war prizes.

Japan realized this. During World War I, Russia and Japan were allies rather than adversaries. As a gesture of solidarity, Japan returned *Tango* (formerly *Poltava*), *Sagami* (formerly *Peresvet*) and *Soya* (formerly *Varyag*) to Imperial Russia. *Tango* was renamed *Chesma*, but the other two resumed brief careers under their original names.

The Japanese captured four Russian battleships and coastal defense ships at Tsushima. The four became part of the Japanese Navy. This shows *Admiral Senyavin* and *General-Admiral Apraksin* entering Japan as prizes flying Japanese flags over Russian flags. (AC)

STATISTICS AND HISTORIES

All measurements are imperial: feet, tons, knots, and horsepower. The Imperial Russian Navy used the British system for ships. Length is length between parallels, unless noted otherwise. Draft is average draft. Displacement is long tons (2,240 pounds). All units are given as designed, with differences (and the reasons for the difference) given in parentheses following the value.

Armament and other data are given as completed unless otherwise noted. The number after the slash in the size of the gun (e,g. 6in./45) is the gun's caliber – the ratio of barrel length to bore. (A 45-caliber 6-inch gun has a barrel length of 270 inches, or 22 feet, 6 inches.) The disposition of the guns in turrets is shown in parenthesis following the size of the gun if the ship has

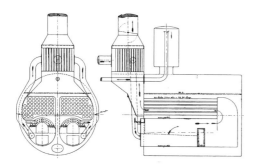

The cylindrical or Scotch boiler was the standard maritime fire-tube boiler. Russian cruisers up to *Rurik* and battleships up the Poltava class used Scotch boilers. (AC)

multiple mounts. Example – 4 x12in. (2x2) means the 12-inch guns are in two two-gun turrets. This is omitted when guns are all single mounts. 3-pounders are 47mm guns. 1-pounders are 37mm guns.

Vessels were coal-fired. Standard and maximum fuel loads are given. As previously mentioned, Russia used the Julian calendar up to the Russian Revolution, but all dates for significant construction milestones are in Gregorian calendar because of space considerations.

There is a great deal of uncertainty in these statistics. Imperial Russia was sloppy about measurement and even sloppier about maintaining records. Record-keeping was complicated by the loss of records during the Revolution and World War II. I have tried to use the best available information, but this information is often contradictory.

Service history is specific to each ship, providing detail absent in the Operational History section.

Battleships

Imperator Nikolai I

Named for Imperator Nikolai I, Tsar of Russia 1825–55. Visited New York City in 1893. In Pacific from 1894–96. In Mediterranean in 1897, supporting rebelling Cretans. Refitted in Kronstadt 1898–99. In Mediterranean 1901– 04. Assigned as flagship of Third Pacific Squadron. At Tsushima (1905), surrendered May 28. Entered Japanese Navy and used as gunnery training ship *Iki* between 1905 and 1910. School ship 1910–15. Stricken from the list in 1915 and sunk as a target.

Displacement	8,440 tons (9,594 actual)
Dimensions	325ft 10in. x 66ft 11in. x 24ft 3in.
Machinery	2 triple-expansion engines (2 shafts), 12 cylindrical boilers, 7,842ihp; coal-fired, 847 tons normal
Max Speed	14.5kts
Armament	Guns: 2 × 12in./30 (2x1), 8 × 9in./35 (4x1) 8 × 6in./35 (8x1), 10 × 5-barrel revolving 3-pounder, 8 × 5-barrel revolving 1-pounder. Torpedo tubes: 6 x 15in.
Armor	Compound armor. Belt: 10–14in., deck: 2.5in., 9-inch gun casemate: 3in., 6-inch gun casemate: 2in., turrets: 10in., conning tower: 10in.
Crew	616
Shipyard	Galeryi. **Laid down**: August 4, 1886. **Launched**: June 1, 1889. **Entered Service**: July 1891

PETROPAVLOVSK

Petropavlovsk was one of three Poltava-class battleships started for the Imperial Russian Navy in the early 1890s. *Petropavlovsk* proved the favorite of the three, serving as the fleet flagship for Russia's Pacific Squadron.

The last class of Russian battleship intended to fight in the Baltic Sea, it marked a transition point in Russian naval architecture, with a combination of old and new. It was the first class to mount secondary armament in turrets, but retained fire-tube boilers. *Poltava* was the first battleship to have Krupp armor, while *Petropavlovsk* used nickel steel and *Sevastopol* had Harvey steel.

Admiral Stepan Makarov used it as his flagship when he took command at Port Arthur. On April 13, 1904, steaming back to port, *Petropavlovsk* struck a mine. The Poltava-class battleships had the forward 12-inch magazines, the torpedo magazine, and a magazine for 50 mines (intended to allow battleships security at unprotected anchorages) located together near the ship's bottom. The mine detonated one magazine, which caused the adjacent munitions to explode, sinking the ship almost instantaneously.

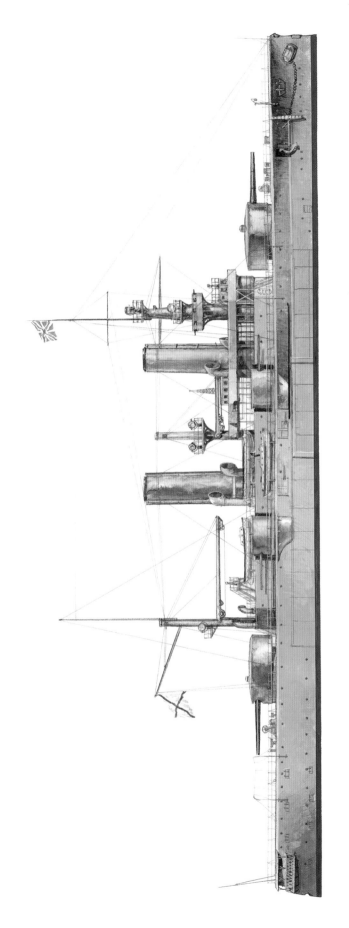
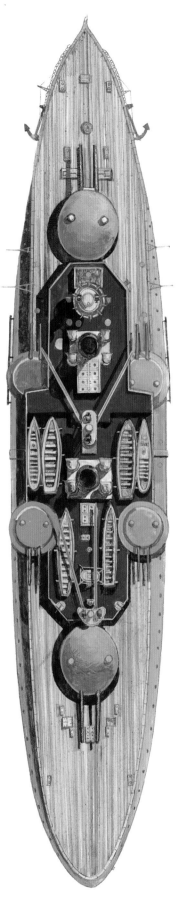

Navarin

Named for the 1827 battle of Navarino. Assigned to Mediterranean 1896–98. Reassigned to Pacific 1898–1902. Under refit in Kronstadt 1902–04. Assigned to Second Pacific Squadron 1904. Mined and sunk at Tsushima.

Displacement	10,206 tons
Dimensions	338ft x 67ft x 27ft 7in.
Machinery	2 triple-expansion engines (2 shafts), 12 cylindrical boilers, 9,000ihp; coal-fired: 700 tons normal, 1,200 tons maximum
Max Speed	14.85kts
Armament	Guns: 4 × 12in./35 (2x2), 8 × 6in./35, 14 × 3-pounder, 12 x 1-pounder. Torpedo tubes: 6 x 15in.
Armor	Compound armor. Belt: 12–16in., deck: 2–3in., casemate: 5in., turrets (nickel steel): 12in., conning tower: 10in.
Crew	441
Shipyard	Admiralty. **Laid down:** May 31, 1890. **Launched**: October 20, 1891. **Entered Service**: June 1895

Sissoi Veliky

Named for Saint Sisoes the Great. Sent to Mediterranean during Cretan Rebellion. Ordered to Far East in 1898, remained through 1901. Refitted in Libau 1901–04. Assigned to Second Pacific Squadron. Torpedoed and sunk at Tsushima.

Displacement	8,800 tons (10,400 actual)
Dimensions	333ft 6in. x 68ft x 25ft 6in
Machinery	2 triple-expansion engines (2 shafts), 12 cylindrical boilers, 8500ihp; coal-fired: 550 tons normal, 1,000 maximum
Max Speed	15.65kts
Armament	Guns: 4 × 12in./40 (2x2), 6 × 6in./45, 12 × 3-pounder, 10 x 1-pounder. Torpedo tubes: 6 x 15in.
Armor	Nickel steel. Belt: 12–16in., deck: 2½–3in., turrets: 10–12in., casemate: 5in., conning tower: 9in.
Crew	686
Shipyard	Admiralty. **Laid down**: May 19, 1892. **Launched**: June 1 ,1894. **Entered Service**: August 30, 1896

The two pairs of side-by-side funnels gave *Navarin* an unmistakable appearance. Because of them, its nickname was "the Factory." (AC)

Poltava class

Poltava: Named for the 1709 Great Northern War battle of Poltava. Pacific Squadron 1899–1904. At battle of Yellow Sea, August 10. Sunk by Japanese 11-inch howitzers in Port Arthur, December 1904. Raised, repaired, and recommissioned by Japan 1905–09 as coast defense ship *Tango*. Participated in siege of Tsingtao and in the Mediterranean during World War I. Returned to Russia in 1916, renamed *Chesma*. Refitted in Great Britain and sent to Murmansk in 1917. Declared for Soviets, seized by British in 1918. Left in Murmansk when abandoned by Britain in 1920. Scrapped 1924.

Petropavlovsk: Named for the Crimean War battle of Petropavlovsk-Kamchatka. Pacific Squadron 1899–1904 as flagship. Engaged Japanese fleet February 9, 1904. Mined and sunk May 7, 1904.

Sevastopol: Named for Sevastopol, a Crimean Peninsula Russian naval port. Pacific Squadron 1900–04. At the battle of the Yellow Sea. Moved to Port Arthur's Outer Harbor to take it out of range of Japanese siege guns attacking Inner Harbor. Unsuccessfully attacked by Japanese torpedo craft. Scuttled in deep water, January 2, 1905 to prevent capture or salvage by Japan.

Petropavlovsk served as the flagship of the Pacific Squadron from its arrival in 1899 until it was sunk in April 1904. (AC)

Poltava class	
Displacement	10,960 tons (11,354–11,842 actual)
Dimensions	356ft x 70ft x 28ft 3in.
Machinery	2 triple-expansion engines (2 shafts), 16 Scotch (cylindrical) boilers, 10,600ihp (designed) 9,368–11,255 (actual); coal-fired: 700 tons normal, 1,050 full load
Max Speed	16kts (15.3–16.4 trials)
Armament	Guns: 4 × 12in./40 (4×2), 12 × 6in./45 (4x2, 4x1), 12 × 3-pounder, 28 x 1-pounder. Torpedo tubes: 4 x 15in., 2 x 18 in. (submerged)
Armor	Nickel steel (*Petropavlovsk*), Harvey steel (*Sevastopol*), Krupp steel (*Poltava*). Belt: 12–16in., deck: 2–3in., main turrets: 10in., barbettes: 10in., secondary turrets: 6in., conning tower: 9in.
Crew	650 (750 as flagship)
Shipyard	*Poltava* – Admiralty, *Petropavlovsk*, *Sevastopol* – Galeryi. Laid down: *Poltava*: May 19, 1892; *Petropavlovsk*: May 19, 1892; *Sevastopol*: May 19, 1892. Launched: *Poltava*: November 6, 1894; *Petropavlovsk*: November 9, 1894; *Sevastopol*: June 1, 1895. Entered Service: *Poltava*, *Petropavlovsk*: 1899; *Sevastopol*: 1900

Peresvet class

Peresvet: Named for 14th-century warrior-monk Alexander Peresvet. Pacific Squadron 1901–04. At Port Arthur and battle of the Yellow Sea. Scuttled in Port Arthur's Inner Harbor after being hit by Japanese 11-inch siege guns. Raised, repaired, and recommissioned by Japan 1905–08 as coast defense ship *Sagami*; served in Japanese Navy 1908–16. Sold back to Russia in 1916. Struck mine and sank off Port Said, January 4, 1917.

Oslyabya: Named for a 14th-century warrior-monk. En route to Port Arthur when the war started. Returned to Baltic. Assigned to Second Pacific Squadron. Sunk at Tsushima.

Pobeda: Russian for "Victory." Pacific Squadron 1903–04. Fought at Port Arthur. Struck mine on May 7, but survived and was repaired. At the battle of the Yellow Sea. Sunk at Port Arthur in December by Japanese siege howitzers. Raised, repaired, and recommissioned by Japan 1905–08 as coast defense ship *Suwo*. Blockaded Tsingtao in 1914. Gunnery training ship 1917–18. Capsized in 1922 while armor was being removed. Broken up 1923.

Peresvet class	
Displacement	12,674 tons (13,320–14,408 tons as built)
Dimensions	401ft 3in. x 71ft 9in. x 26ft 3in.
Machinery	3 vertical triple-expansion engines (3 shafts), 30 Belleville boilers, 14,500ihp; coal-fired: 1,060 tons normal, 2,030 maximum
Max Speed	18kts (18.3–18.5 trials)
Armament	Guns: 4 × 10in./45 (2x2), 11 × 6in./45, 20 x 3in./50, 20 x 3-pounder, 8 x 1-pounder. Torpedo tubes: 5 x 15in. (two submerged)
Armor	Harvey steel (*Peresvet*, *Oslyabya*), Krupp steel (*Pobeda*). Belt: 4–9in., deck: 2–3in., casemates: 5in., turrets: 9in., conning tower: 6in.
Crew	771
Shipyard	*Peresvet*, *Pobeda* – Baltic; *Oslyabya* – Admiralty. Laid down: *Peresvet*, *Oslyabya*: November 21, 1895; *Pobeda*: February 21, 1899. Launched: *Peresvet*: May 19, 1898; *Oslyabya*: November 8, 1898; *Pobeda*: May 10, 1900. Entered Service: *Peresvet*: 1901, *Oslyabya*: 1903, *Pobeda*: 1902

Retvizan

Named for Swedish warship *Rättvisa*, "Justice," captured in 1790. Pacific Squadron 1902–04. Torpedoed during opening day surprise attack. Repaired; at the battle of the Yellow Sea. Sunk at Port Arthur in December by Japanese siege howitzers. Raised, repaired, and recommissioned by Japan 1905–08 as coast defense ship *Hizen*. Participated in World War I and Russian Civil War in the Pacific. Stricken 1923. Sunk as gunnery target 1924.

CHARGE OF THE *RETVIZAN* AT THE BATTLE OF THE YELLOW SEA

On August 10, 1904, the First Pacific Squadron attempted a breakout to Vladivostok. Late that afternoon it looked as if the Russian fleet would successfully escape. Thirty minutes before sunset, however, the flagship *Tsesarevich* was hit by two 12in. shells. One hit the bridge, killing the admiral commanding the fleet, the command staff and the helmsman. The second hit the rudder, putting the ship in a tight circle. Following the uncommanded flagship caused the Russian formation to disintegrate. As most of the Russian fleet milled about in confusion, the Japanese, seeing this confusion, closed on *Tsesarevich* to sink it.

The captain of the battleship *Retvizan*, Eduard Schensnovich, decided to protect *Tsesarevich*. He turned *Retvizan* towards the Japanese battle line, conducting a lone battleship charge against the entire Japanese fleet. A hurricane of shells rained down as *Retvizan* became the target of four Japanese battleships and two large armored cruisers. The shells fell so thick Japanese ships could not determine which shell splashes were theirs and which were due to other ships. This prevented these ships from correcting errors. They also could not tell whether their shells were landing over *Retvizan* or short of it.

The charge succeeded in drawing Japanese attention away from *Tsesarevich* and caused the Japanese to move their battle line away from the Russian fleet. *Tsesarevich* reached the safety of Tsingtao after night fell. Although Captain Schensnovich was wounded and *Retvizan* hit 18 times, the ship escaped serious damage. As darkness fell, *Retvizan* rejoined the Russian battle line, now under command of Admiral Pavel Ukhtomsky, and was able to steam back to Port Arthur that evening.

This plate shows *Retvizan* as it charges into the Japanese surrounded by shell splashes, with the Russian battle line in the background.

Displacement	12,746 tons (12,900 tons actual).
Dimensions	376ft x 72ft 2in. x 25ft
Machinery	2 vertical triple-expansion engines (2 shafts), 24 Niclausse water-tube boilers, 17,112shp; coal-fired: 1,616 tons normal, 2,000 maximum
Max Speed	18kts
Armament	Guns: 4 × 12in./40 (2x2), 12 × 6in./40, 20 × 3in./50, 24 × 3-pounder, 6 x 1-pounder. Torpedo tubes: 6 x 15in. (2 submerged)
Armor	Krupp armor. Belt: 5–9in., deck: 2–3in., casemate: 5in., main turrets: 9in., conning tower: 10in.
Crew	750
Shipyard	Cramp. **Laid down:** 29 July 1899. **Launched:** 23 October 1900. **Entered Service:** 23 March 1902

Tsesarevich

Named for the heir to the Imperial Russian throne. Arrived at Port Arthur in November 1903. Torpedoed and damaged during opening day surprise attack. Repaired. At the battle of the Yellow Sea as Admiral Vitgeft's flagship. Escaped to Tsingtao after battle; interned. Reassigned to Baltic after war, conducting annual Mediterranean winter cruises between 1906 and 1913. In Baltic during World War I. Renamed *Grazhdanin* (Citizen) after October Revolution. Damaged at battle of Moonsund October 1917, and laid up afterwards. Scrapped 1925.

Displacement	12,915 tons (13,110 actual)
Dimensions	372ft x 76ft 1in. x 26ft
Machinery	2 vertical triple-expansion engines (2 shafts), 20 Belleville boilers, 16,300ihp (16,500ihp at speed trials); coal-fired: 800 tons normal, 1,350 maximum
Max Speed	18kts (18.77 trials)
Armament	Guns: 4 × 12in./40 (2×2), 12 × 6in./45 (6x2), 20 × 3in./50, 20 × 3-pounder, 8 x 1-pounder. Torpedo tubes: 6 x 15in. (two submerged)
Armor	Krupp armor. Belt: 6.7–9.84in., deck: 2in., barbettes: 9.84in., main turrets: 9.84in., secondary turrets: 5.9in., conning tower: 10in. forward, 9in. aft
Crew	732
Shipyard	La Seyne. **Laid down:** July 8, 1899. **Launched:** February 23, 1901. **Entered Service:** August 31, 1903

Pobeda was one of three "cruiser-battleships" built for the Imperial Russian Navy. Sunk in Port Arthur, it was later refloated by Japan and repaired, serving in the Japanese Navy for 14 years. (AC)

Borodino class

Borodino: Named for the 1812 battle of Borodino. Assigned to Second Pacific Squadron in 1904. Sunk at Tsushima.

Imperator Aleksander III: Named for Aleksander III, Tsar of Russia 1881–94. Assigned to Second Pacific Squadron in 1904. Sunk at Tsushima.

Knyaz Suvorov: Named for Knyaz (Prince) Alexander Vasilyevich Suvorov. Assigned to Second Pacific Squadron in 1904. Sunk at Tsushima.

Oryol: Eagle in Russian. Assigned to Second Pacific Squadron in 1904. Surrendered at Tsushima. Refitted by Japan. Commissioned in Japanese Navy as *Iwami* in 1907. Rated as a coastal defense ship in 1912. Served in Pacific during World War I and Russian Revolution, participating in siege of Tsingtao and Japanese Russian Intervention. Training ship in 1921. Stricken 1922. Sunk as a target or scrapped in 1924.

Coastal Defense Ships
Admiral Ushakov class
Admiral Ushakov: Named for Fyodor Ushakov, a late 18th-century Russian admiral. Served in Baltic 1895–1904. Assigned to Third Pacific Squadron. Sunk at Tsushima.

Admiral Senyavin: Named for Dmitry Senyavin, Russian fleet commander at Navarino. Served in Baltic 1896–1904. Assigned to Third Pacific Squadron. Surrendered at Tsushima. Commissioned in Imperial Japanese Navy as coastal defense ship *Mishima*. At Siege of Tsingtao and Japanese Russian Intervention during World War I and Russian Civil War. Rerated submarine tender 1921. Struck from Japanese Navy in 1935. Sunk as target September 1936.

Abandoned by the rest of the Pacific Squadron after the battle of the Yellow Sea, *Tsesarevich* steamed to Tsingtao, where it was interned until the war ended. This picture shows *Tsesarevich* at Tsingtao shortly after its arrival. It was the only Russian battleship in the Pacific to avoid capture or destruction. (AC)

Admiral Ushakov class	
Displacement	4,126 tons
Dimensions	265ft x 52ft 6in. x 17ft
Machinery	2 vertical triple-expansion engines (2 shafts), 8 (*Ushavkov* 4) cylindrical boilers, 5,750ihp; coal-fired: 450 tons
Max Speed	16kts
Armament	Guns: 4 × 10in./40 (2x2), 4 × 4.7in./40, 6 × 3-pounder, 10 x 1-pounder. Torpedo tubes: 4 x 15in.
Armor	Compound armor. Belt: 10in., deck: 3in., main turrets: 8in., conning tower: 8in.
Crew	400
Shipyard	*Admiral Ushakov* – Admiralty; *Admiral Senyavin* – Baltic. Laid down: *Ushakov*: January 13, 1892; *Senyavin*: August, 1892. Launched: *Ushakov*: November 12, 1893; *Senyavin*: September 2, 1894. Entered Service: *Ushakov*: 1895; *Senyavin*: 1896

The battleship *Oryol* in the Baltic shortly after it was commissioned. The only Borodino-class battleship to survive Tsushima, it was captured along with three other Russian warships. (AC)

General-Admiral Apraksin

Named for Fyodor Apraksin, one of Russia's first admirals. Baltic Fleet 1899 through 1904. Ran aground in 1899, but salvaged. Assigned to Third Pacific Squadron. Surrendered at Tsushima. Commissioned as Imperial Japanese Navy coastal defense ship *Okinoshima*. At Tsingtao and Japanese Russian Intervention during World War I and Russian Civil War. Rerated a submarine tender in 1921. Struck from Japanese Navy 1922. Sold 1924; transformed into a museum ship. Finally scrapped in 1939.

Displacement	4,165 tons.
Dimensions	264ft 6in. x 52ft x 17ft
Machinery	2 vertical triple-expansion engines (2 shafts), 4 cylindrical boilers, 6,000ihp; coal-fired: 215 tons normal, 313 maximum
Max Speed	15kts
Armament	Guns: 3 × 10in./40 (1x2, 1x1), 4 × 4.7in./40, 10 × 3-pounder, 12 x 1-pounder. Torpedo tubes; 4 x 15in.
Armor	Compound armor. Belt: 10in., deck: 3in., main turrets: 8in., conning tower: 8in.
Crew	318
Shipyard	Admiralty. **Laid down:** November 6, 1894. **Launched:** May 25, 1896. **Entered Service:** 1899

Cruisers

Vladimir Monomakh

Named for Vladimir II, a 12th-century Kievan Grand Prince. Far East 1884–87. Refitted at Kronstadt. Mediterranean 1889, Far East 1890–1892. After major refit in Kronstadt, returned briefly to Mediterranean in 1894. Sent to Far East during Sino-Japanese War. Major refit at Kronstadt, 1896. Far East service 1897–1902. Refitted 1903–04. Assigned to Third Pacific Squadron. Sunk at Tsushima.

Displacement	6,061 tons
Dimensions	296ft 6in. x 52ft x 24ft
Machinery	2 compound engines (2 shafts), 12 Scotch (cylindrical) boilers, 7,000ihp; coal-fired: 9,400 tons
Max Speed	15.2kts
Armament	Guns: 5 × 6in./45 (5x1), 6 × 4.7in., 6 × 3-pounder, 10 x 1-pounder. Torpedo tubes: 3 x 15in. (after 1896 refit)
Armor	Compound armor. Belt: 4.75-9in., deck: 3in., casemate: 3–4in.
Crew	550
Shipyard	Baltic. **Laid down:** February 22, 1881. **Launched:** October 22, 1882. **Entered Service:** 1884

Dmitrii Donskoi

Named for Dmitry Donskoy, a 14th-century Prince of Moscow and Grand Prince of Vladimir. Mediterranean service 1885–87. Far East 1887–89. Refitted in Kronstadt 1800–91. Far East 1891–93. Visited US in 1893. Refitted at Kronstadt 1893–95, when rearmed. Far East 1896–1901. Refitted at Kronstadt 1902–03. Heading to Port Arthur when war started, returned to Baltic. Assigned to Second Pacific Squadron. Sunk at Tsushima.

The coast defense ship *Admiral Senyavin* in the Baltic. Due to their low freeboard *Senyavin*, *Ushakov* and *Apraksin* were called the "flatirons" by the Russian Navy's sailors. (AC)

Displacement	5,882 tons
Dimensions	296ft 5in. x 52ft x 24ft 9in.
Machinery	2 compound engines (2 shafts), 6 Scotch (cylindrical) boilers, 7,000ihp; coal-fired: 900 tons
Max Speed	16.5kts
Armament	Guns: 6 × 6in./35, 10 × 4.7in., 6 × 3-pounder, 10 x 1-pounder. Torpedo tubes: 4 x 15in.
Armor	Compound armor. Belt: 4.5–9in., deck: ½in., barbettes: 3–4in.
Crew	510
Shipyard	Admiralty. **Laid down:** May 21, 1881. **Launched:** August 30, 1883. **Entered Service:** 1886

Admiral Nakhimov

Named for Pavel Nakhimov, Sevastopol commander during Crimean War siege. Flagship Vladivostok Squadron 1888–1891. Refitted Baltic, 1891. Visited France and US in 1893. Far East 1894–98. Modernized in Baltic 1898–99. Far East 1899–1903. Awaiting refit at Kronstadt 1903–04. Assigned to Second Pacific Squadron. Sunk at Tsushima.

Displacement	8,524 tons
Dimensions	333ft x 61ft x 25ft
Machinery	2 vertical triple-expansion engines (2 shafts), 12 cylindrical boilers, 9,000ihp; coal-fired: 1,200 tons
Max Speed	17kts
Armament	Guns: 8 × 8in./35 (4x2), 10 × 6in./35, 4 × 4.1in./40, 15 × 3-pounder. Torpedo tubes: 3 x 15in.
Armor	Compound armor. Belt: 10in., deck: 2–3in, turrets: 2–2½in., barbettes: 8in., conning tower: 6in.
Crew	517
Shipyard	Baltic. **Laid down:** July 1884. **Launched:** October 1885. **Entered Service:** September 1888

Rurik

Named for the Kievan-Rus dynasty's founder, King Rurik. Represented Russia at 1895 Kiel Canal opening. Far East 1895–1904. Refitted

1900–01 in Vladivostok. Served in Vladivostok Independent Cruiser Squadron during the Russo-Japanese War. Sunk at the Battle of Uslan, August 14, 1904.

Displacement	10,923 tons (11,690 actual)
Dimensions	412ft x 67ft x 26ft
Machinery	4 vertical triple-expansion engines (2 shafts), 8 cylindrical boilers, 13,250ihp; coal-fired: 1,933 tons
Max Speed	18kts (18.8 trials)
Armament	Guns: 4 × 8in./35, 16 × 6in./45, 6 × 4.7in./43, 6 × 3-pounder, 10 x 1-pounder. Torpedo tubes: 6 x 15in.
Armor	Nickel steel. Belt: 8–10.8in., deck: 3in., conning tower: 6in.
Crew	719
Shipyard	Baltic. **Laid down:** May 31, 1890. **Launched:** November 3, 1892. **Entered Service:** May 1895

Rossia

Named for Russia. Attended Queen Victoria's Diamond Jubilee in 1897. Flagship of Vladivostok Cruiser Squadron 1897–1905. Participated in seven raids during Russo-Japanese War; badly damaged at battle of Uslan. Returned to Kronstadt after the War, refitted, and served as flagship of Baltic 2nd Cruiser Brigade in World War I. Inactive during Russian Revolution. Scrapped in Germany in 1922.

Displacement	12,130 tons (12,195 actual)
Dimensions	461ft x 68ft 7in. x 26ft 2in.
Machinery	3 vertical triple-expansion engines (3 shafts), 32 Belleville boilers, 14,500ihp; coal-fired: 1,933 tons
Max Speed	19kts (19.75 trials)
Armament	Guns: 4 × 8in./45, 16 × 6in./45, 12 × 3in./50, 20 × 3-pounder, 18 x 1-pounder. Torpedo tubes: 5 x 15in.
Armor	Harvey steel. Belt: 6½–8in., deck: 2½–3in., conning tower: 12in.
Crew	839
Shipyard	Baltic. **Laid down:** June 1, 1895. **Launched:** May 12, 1896. **Entered Service:** Late 1896

Svetlana

Royal yacht for Grand Duke Alexei and Imperial family, 1899–1903. Assigned to Second Pacific Squadron in 1904. Sunk day after Tsushima, attempting to reach Vladivostok.

Displacement	3,828 tons
Dimensions	331ft 3in. x 42ft 9in. x 18ft 9in.
Machinery	2 vertical triple-expansion engines (2 shafts), 18 Belleville boilers, 8,500ihp; coal-fired: 1,000 tons
Max Speed	18kts (20.2 trials)
Armament	Guns: 6 × 6in./45, 10 × 3-pounder. Torpedo tubes: 2 x 15in.
Armor	Harvey steel. Deck: 1–2in., gun shields: 4in., conning tower: 4in.
Crew	360
Shipyard	Le Havre. **Laid down:** December 8, 1895. **Launched:** October 7, 1896. **Entered Service:** 1897

Rossia served as the flagship for the Vladivostok Independent Cruiser Squadron from 1897 though 1905. Its wartime battle damage was repaired in Kronstadt after the war ended. (AC)

Pallada class

Pallada: Named for Pallas Athena, Greek goddess of war and wisdom. Pacific Squadron 1902–04. Torpedoed at Port Arthur, February 8–9, and at battle of Yellow Sea, but repaired both times. Sunk by 11-inch howitzers at Port Arthur, December 1904. Raised, repaired, and recommissioned by Japan 1905–08. Served as Japanese training ship *Tsugaru* 1908–20. Scuttled 1922.

Diana: Named for the Roman goddess of the hunt. Pacific Squadron 1902–04. At battle of Yellow Sea, escaped to Saigon. Returned to Baltic after war. Served in 2nd Cruiser Brigade in World War I. Joined revolutionary forces in 1917, in Revolutionary navy 1917–21. Scrapped, Germany, 1922.

Aurora: Named for the goddess of the dawn. Going to Port Arthur when war started; returned to Baltic. Assigned to Second Pacific Squadron. At Tsushima, escaped to Manila and interned. Returned to Baltic after war. Served in Baltic during World War I. Joined revolutionary forces in 1917. In reserve 1918. Training ship 1922–41. Disarmed during World War II, sunk in port. Refloated and refitted as museum ship, 1945–47. Currently museum ship in St Petersburg.

Pallada class	
Displacement	6,657–6,897 tons.
Dimensions	413ft 3in. x 55ft 9in. x 21ft
Machinery	3 vertical triple-expansion engines (3 shafts), 24 Belleville boilers, 11,600ihp; coal-fired: 900 tons normal, 1,400 maximum
Max Speed	19kts
Armament	Guns: 8 × 6.in/45, 24 x 3in./50, 8 x 1-pounder. Torpedo tubes: 3 x 15in.
Armor	Harvey steel. Deck: 2–4in., guns: 4in., conning tower: 6in.
Crew	580
Shipyard	Admiralty. **Laid down:** *Pallada*: December 13, 1895; *Diana*: June 4, 1897; *Aurora*: June 4, 1897. **Launched:** *Pallada*: August 1899; *Diana*: October 12, 1899; *Aurora*: June 24, 1900. **Entered Service:** *Pallada*: 1901; *Diana*: December 1901; *Aurora*: 1903

Gromboi

Russian for thunderer. Far East, 1900–05. In Vladivostok Cruiser Squadron during Russo-Japanese War. Badly damaged at battle of Uslan. Repaired but ran aground on trial run; inactive for rest of war. Returned to Baltic after war, and refitted. Served in 2nd Cruiser Brigade in World War I. Scrapped in Germany, 1922.

Displacement	12,360 tons (12,455 actual)
Dimensions	461ft x 68ft 6in. x 26ft
Machinery	3 vertical triple-expansion engines (3 shafts), 32 Belleville boilers, 14,500ihp; coal-fired: 2,400 tons
Max Speed	19kts (20.1 trials)
Armament	Guns: 4 × 8in./45, 16 × 6in./45, 24 × 3in./50, 12 × 3-pounder, 18 x 1-pounder. Torpedo tubes: 4 x 15in.
Armor	Harvey steel. Belt: 6in., deck: 1½–2.5in, casemates: 4.76in., conning tower: 12in.
Crew	874
Shipyard	Baltic. **Laid down:** May 19, 1898. **Launched:** May 20, 1899. **Entered Service:** November 1900

Svetlana was officially a protected cruiser, and carried both guns and armor. In reality she was built to serve as a yacht for the Imperial Royal Family. She was hunted down and sunk by the Japanese on May 26, 1905. (USNHHC)

Boyarin was the shortest-lived and least lucky cruiser in the Russian Navy. After less than two years' service it struck a friendly mine and sank. Built in Denmark, it was viewed as an unsatisfactory design. (USNHHC)

Bayan

Named for an 11th-century Russian bard. Pacific Squadron 1903–04. Sunk in harbor by 11-inch Japanese howitzers, December 1904. Raised, repaired, and recommissioned by Japan 1905–08. Training ship *Aso* in Japanese Navy 1908–1920; minelayer 1920–30. Sunk as gunnery target 1932.

Displacement	7,725 tons (7,802 actual)
Dimensions	443ft x 57ft 6in. x 22ft
Machinery	2 vertical triple-expansion engines (2 shafts), 26 Belleville boilers, 17,400ihp; coal-fired: 1,200 tons maximum
Max Speed	21kts
Armament	Guns: 2 x 8in./45, 8 × 6in./45, 20 x 3in./50, 8 x 3-pounder, 2 x 1-pounder. Torpedo tubes: 6 x 15in.
Armor	Harvey steel. Belt: 3.9–7.9in., deck: 2in., barbettes: 6.7in., casemates: 2.4in. turrets: 5.9in., conning tower: 6.3in.
Crew	573
Shipyard	La Seyne. **Laid down:** March 1899. **Launched:** June 12, 1900. **Entered Service:** December 1902

Askold

Named for Askold, prince of Kiev and founder of the first Viking state in Dnieper. Pacific Squadron 1902–04. At battle of Yellow Sea, escaped to Shanghai. Pacific Fleet flagship 1908–14. In Mediterranean 1914–16 during World War I. Barents Sea flotilla 1917–18 as part of Provisional Government. Seized by Great Britain after Russian Revolution. Released in 1922 and sold for scrap.

Displacement	6100 tons
Dimensions	426ft 3in. x 49ft 3in. x 20ft 9in.
Machinery	3 vertical triple-expansion engines (2 shafts), 9 Schultz-Thornycroft boilers, 24,000ihp; coal-fired: 720 tons normal, 1,100 maximum
Max Speed	23.8kts
Armament	Guns: 12 × 6in./45, 12 x 3in./50 8 × 3-pounder, 2 x 1-pounder. Torpedo tubes: 6 x 15in.
Armor	Krupp steel. Deck: 2–4in., guns: 4in., conning tower: 6in.
Crew	580
Shipyard	Germaniawerft. **Laid down:** June 8, 1899. **Launched:** March 2, 1900. **Entered Service:** January 1902

The cruiser *Askold* was the fastest cruiser in the Imperial Russian Navy. Its five funnels gave it a distinctive appearance, but it was viewed as an inferior design to that of *Bogatyr*. (AC)

Varyag

Named after the Varangian or Viking people. Pacific Squadron 1901–04. Scuttled in Chemulpo after a battle with a Japanese squadron, February 9, 1904. Raised, repaired, and recommissioned by Japan 1904–07. Third-class cruiser *Soya* in Japanese Navy 1907–16. Returned to Russia April 1916, original name restored. Departed Vladivostok for refit in Great Britain. Seized by British after October Revolution. Ran aground off Ireland in 1919 and refloated. Scrapped in Germany 1922.

Displacement	6,500 tons
Dimensions	420ft x 52ft x 20ft 9in.
Machinery	2 vertical triple-expansion engines (2 shafts), 30 Niclausse boilers, 20,000ihp; coal-fired: 770 tons normal, 1,250 maximum
Max Speed	23kts
Armament	Guns: 12 × 6in./45, 12 x 3in./50, 8 × 3-pounder, 2 x 1-pounder. Torpedo tubes: 6 x 15in.
Armor	Krupp steel. Deck: 3in., turrets: 5in., conning tower: 5.5in.
Crew	571
Shipyard	Cramp. **Laid down:** October 1898. **Launched:** October 31, 1899. **Entered Service:** January 1901

Bogatyr class

Bogatyr: A Russian form of Hercules. Vladivostok Cruiser Squadron 1903–05. Participated in two cruiser sweeps during Russo-Japanese War. Struck a rock in May 1904; in Vladivostok awaiting repair the rest of the war. Reassigned to Baltic after the war. In Mediterranean 1908. Refitted in 1912. In Baltic 1st Cruiser Squadron during World War I. Declared for Revolutionaries in 1917. Scrapped in Germany 1922.

Oleg: Named for Oleg of Novgorod, a late 9th-century Varangian prince. Assigned to Second Pacific Squadron upon commissioning. At Tsushima, escaped to Manila and interned. In Baltic after war, under refit 1905–08. In Baltic 1st Cruiser Squadron in World War I. Declared for Revolutionaries in 1917. Torpedoed and sunk by British torpedo boat June 17, 1919.

Bogatyr class	
Displacement	6,645 tons (*Oleg*: 6,675).
Dimensions	416ft 9in. x 54ft 6in. x 20ft 9in. (*Oleg*: 439ft 9in. x 51ft 6in. x 20ft 6in.)
Machinery	2 vertical triple-expansion engines (2 shafts), 16 Normand-style boilers, 23,000ihp; coal-fired: 720 tons normal, 1,100 max
Max Speed	23kts (23.4 trials)
Armament	Guns: 12 × 6in./45 (2x2, 8x1), 12 x 3in./50, 8 × 3-pounder, 2 x 1-pounder. Torpedo tubes: 4 x 15in. (2 submerged) (*Oleg*: 2 x 15in. (submerged))
Armor	Krupp steel. Deck: 3in., casemates: 3in., turrets: 5in., conning tower: 5½in.
Crew	580
Shipyard	*Bogatyr* – Vulkan; *Oleg* – Admiralty. **Laid down:** *Bogatyr*: December 22, 1899; *Oleg*: July 6, 1902. **Launched:** *Bogatyr*: July 30, 1901; *Oleg*: August 14, 1903. **Entered Service:** *Bogatyr*: 1902; *Oleg*: June 24, 1904

Novik

Russian term for a young noble or boyar. Pacific Squadron 1902–04. Participated in several sweeps from Port Arthur February through June 1904. At battle of Yellow Sea, escaped to Tsingtao, coaled, and attempted to reach Vladivostok. Trapped by Japanese in Aniva Bay, Sakhalin Island. Scuttled August 20. Raised, repaired, and recommissioned by Japan 1905–06. Japanese cruiser *Suzuya* 1906–12. Scrapped 1913.

Displacement	3,080 tons
Dimensions	347ft 9in. x 41ft 6in. x 16ft
Machinery	3 vertical triple-expansion engines (3 shafts), 12 Schultz-Thornycroft boilers, 18,000ihp; coal-fired: 600 tons
Max Speed	25kts
Armament	Guns: 6 × 4.7in./45, 8 × 3-pounder, 2 x 1-pounder. Torpedo tubes: 6 x 15in.
Armor	Krupp steel. Deck: 2in., conning tower: 1in.
Crew	340
Shipyard	Schichau Shipyard, Bremerhaven, Germany. **Laid down:** February 1900. **Launched:** August 2, 1900. **Entered Service:** May 1902

Boyarin

A member of the highest rank of feudal Russian aristocracy, ranking just below a prince. Pacific Squadron 1902–04. Struck and sunk by a Russian mine off Port Arthur, February 12, 1904.

Displacement	3,200 tons
Dimensions	347ft 9in. x 41ft 6in. x 16ft
Machinery	2 vertical triple-expansion engines (2 shafts), 16 Belleville boilers, 18,800ihp; coal-fired: 600 tons
Max Speed	25kts
Armament	Guns: 6 × 4.7in./45, 8 × 3-pounder, 2 x 1-pounder. Torpedo tubes: 5 x 15in.
Armor	Krupp steel. Deck: 2in., conning tower: 3in.
Crew	334
Shipyard	B&W. **Laid down:** September 24, 1900. **Launched:** May 26, 1901, **Entered Service:** September 1, 1902

Pallada was the first of three domestically designed small protected cruisers in the Russian Navy. It was at Port Arthur when the war started, was sunk near the end of the siege, and later repaired, and served in the Japanese Navy. (AC)

Izumrud class

Izumrud: Russian for emerald. Assigned to Pacific Squadron in 1904. At Tsushima. Ran aground and wrecked off Vladivostok after battle.

Zhemchug: Russian for pearl. Assigned Second Pacific Squadron in 1904. At Tsushima, escaped to Manila and interned. In Pacific 1905–14. Sunk at battle of Penang, October 28, 1914.

Displacement	3,080 tons.
Dimensions	347ft 9in. x 41ft 6in. x 16ft
Machinery	3 vertical triple-expansion engines (3 shafts), 16 Yarrow boilers, 17,000ihp; coal-fired: 600 tons
Max Speed	24kts
Armament	Guns: 8 × 4.7in./45, 4 × 3-pounder, 2 x 1-pounder. Torpedo tubes: 4 x 18in.
Armor	Krupp steel. Belt: 1.3in.; deck: 2in.
Crew	350
Shipyard	Nevsky. **Laid down:** *Izumrud*: January 14, 1901; *Zhemchug*: February 1, 1901. **Launched:** *Izumrud*: October 14, 1903; *Zhemchug*: September 6, 1903. **Entered Service:** *Izumrud*: January 1904; *Zhemchug*: July 1904

Almaz

Russian for diamond. 2nd Pacific Squadron in 1904. At Tsushima, reached Vladivostok. Assigned to the Black Sea Fleet. Converted to seaplane carrier, 1915. Bolshevik headquarters ship during revolution. Seized by French at Odessa; sailed to Algiers in 1920 by White Russian forces. Seized by France in 1928. Scrapped 1934.

Displacement	2,385 tons
Dimensions	363ft x 43ft 6in. x 17ft 6in.
Machinery	Two Triple-expansion engines (2 shafts), 16 Belleville boilers, 7,500ihp; coal-fired: 560 tons
Max Speed	19kts
Armament	Guns: 6 x 4.7in., 8 × 3-pounder, 2 x 1-pounder. Torpedo tubes: 6 x 15in. torpedo tubes (6x1)
Armor	Krupp steel. Deck: 2½in.
Crew	340
Shipyard	Baltic. **Laid down:** October 8, 1902. **Launched:** June 15, 1903. **Entered Service:** December 1903

BIBLIOGRAPHY

Brassey, Thomas (1910), later Viscount Hyth (1911–13), editor, *The Naval Annual*, 1896, 1897, 1898, 1900, 1902, 1903, 1904, 1905, J. Griffin and Co. (Portsmouth, 1896–1906)

Brown, David K., *Warrior to Dreadnought: Warship Development 1860–1905*, Chatham Publishing (London, 1997)

Jane, Fred T., *The Imperial Russian Navy: Its Past, Present, And Future*, W. Thacker & Co. (London, 1899)

Klado, Nicolas, *The Battle of the Sea of Japan*, Hurst and Blackett, Ltd (London, 1906)

McLaughlin, Stephen, *Russian and Soviet Battleships*, Naval Institute Press (Annapolis, MD, 2003)

McLaughlin, Stephen, "From Ruirik to Ruirik: Russia's Armoured Cruisers," *Warship 1999–2000*, Conway Maritime Press (London, 1999)

N.A. *Cassell's History of the Russo-Japanese War* (5 volumes), Cassell and Company (London, Paris, New York and Melbourne, 1905)

Watts, Anthony J., *The Imperial Russian Navy*, Arms & Armour (London,1990)

INDEX